Marketing Yourself
and Your Career

Jane Ballback
Jan Slater

Richard Chang Associates, Inc.
Publications Division
Irvine, California

Marketing Yourself and Your Career

Jane Ballback
Jan Slater

Copyright © 1996 by Richard Chang Associates, Inc.
Printed in the United States of America

All rights reserved. No part of this publication may be reproduced, stored in a retrieval system, or transmitted in any form or by any means—electronic, mechanical, photocopying, recording, or otherwise—without the prior written permission of the publisher.

Library of Congress Catalog Card Number 96-85830

ISBN 1-883553-78-4

First edition

The individuals and events in the case stories throughout this book are real. Names have been changed to protect their privacy.

RICHARD CHANG ASSOCIATES

Richard Chang Associates, Inc.
Publications Division
15265 Alton Parkway, Suite 300
Irvine, CA 92618
(800) 756-8096   (714) 727-7477   Fax (714) 727-7007

Acknowledgments

This book has been fifteen years in the making. We kept waiting for the *"right"* time to begin the writing process. That time never seemed to come, so our first acknowledgments are to Richard Chang and his many talented associates for moving this process along.

We taught ourselves this career development content through our own career and life experiences, by reading a wide variety of business, psychological, financial planning, and career books, and through our partnership of many years with Dr. Ann Coil, a creative and talented program developer and writer.

Our *"real"* teachers, though, were the thousands of clients who attended our workshops and visited our offices with their career challenges and dilemmas. Just when we thought we had heard it all, we would meet someone who had a new and unique story and had the courage and desire to learn something new about themselves and the world of work.

In addition, we would like to thank the many organizations who allowed us to come into their environments to assist in making their specific situation a win-win for everyone involved.

Last, but not least, thanks to Steve and Dennis for their unfailing support of us and the work that we do.

Additional Credits

Edited by Ruth Stingley

Reviewed by Denise Jeffrey

Graphic Layout by Christina Slater

Cover Design by John Odam Design Associates

Preface

Today we are faced with constant changes and increasing challenges that affect our personal and professional lives. Depending on how we address these changes and challenges, they can either be obstacles to growth or opportunities for advancement.

The advantage will belong to those with a commitment to continuous and advantageous learning. The goal of the Publications Division of Richard Chang Associates, Inc. is to provide individuals and organizations with a variety of practical and innovative resources for continuous learning and measurable improvement results.

It is with this goal in mind that we bring you the *Personal Growth and Development Collection*. These books provide realistic and proven advice, techniques, and tools—on a wide range of subjects—to build performance capabilities and achieve lasting results in your personal and professional life.

We hope that once you've had an opportunity to benefit from the *Personal Growth and Development Collection*, and any of the publications available in our *Practical Guidebook Collection*, you will share your thoughts and suggestions with us. We've included a brief Evaluation and Feedback Form at the end of the book that you can fax or send to us.

With your feedback, we can continuously improve the resources we are providing through the Publications Division of Richard Chang Associates, Inc.

Wishing you successful reading,

Richard Y. Chang
President and CEO
Richard Chang Associates, Inc.

Contents

1. Doesn't It Sound Like Bragging? 1

Where Did You Pick Up Your Attitude About Self Marketing?
Why Don't You Self Market?
Self Marketing Is the Way to Go

2. Making Sense of the Marketing Mix 11

What Is Marketing Anyway?
How Does the Marketing Mix Relate to Your Career Development?

3. Jump-Starting the Self-Marketing Process 21

Why Create a "Product" Package
Putting Together an "I Love Me" File
Hitting Your Target with Bullet Statements
Using Your Product Knowledge
Setting the Right Price for Yourself

4. Techniques and Strategies for Being in the Right Place at the Right Time 45

Taking Advantage of Your Current Activities and Contacts
Where Do You Hang Out?

5. Presenting Yourself in a Positive Manner 57

Using the Power of Words to Gain a New Image and Visibility
Creating Self-Marketing Scripts
Upgrading Your Personal Presentation

6. **Promoting Yourself within Your Own Organization** 83

   Making a Lateral Move
   The Realities of Climbing the Ladder
   Working Smart and Getting Where You Want to Be
   Career Conversations with Your Manager
   Marketing Strategies That Work

Chapter 1 Key Points

- Your attitude about marketing yourself is learned from your parents
- Most people can identify with at least four out of the five major reasons why people don't market themselves
- Marketing yourself is not bragging; instead, it's essential for anyone interested in career freedom and advancement

Doesn't It Sound Like Bragging?

1

It was one of those days. Jerry sat at his desk, working diligently on a new project, when Sylvia appeared behind him, obviously excited. "Guess what?" she whispered hurriedly. Jerry raised his eyebrows, but before he could speak, Sylvia said, "I got the promotion!" Jerry mumbled his congratulations, then thought to himself, "Why did she get the promotion? It just doesn't make sense. Sylvia's a good worker, but I work much harder. Besides, I've accomplished more and haven't even missed a day's work in three years. It's just not fair. Sylvia tells everybody about her work successes, but my work, which is better, definitely speaks for itself. Couldn't the boss see that I should get the promotion?" Jerry mulled over the situation all day long. He had been hoping for that same promotion. But what Jerry couldn't quite conceptualize was that good work plus great marketing skills always wins out over extra-good work and no marketing skills. Sylvia knew how to market herself. Jerry didn't. And that one difference kept Jerry tethered to the same position while catapulting Sylvia up the career ladder.

> "If you think you can do a thing or think you can't do a thing, you're right."
> Henry Ford

Whom do you identify with? Are you like Jerry, reluctant to articulate your skills and accomplishments, or do you take after Sylvia—well-versed in marketing yourself? It could mean the difference between career frustration and career success. Marketing yourself and your career puts you on the fast track to success. If you learn, practice, and become skillful in marketing yourself and your career, you'll find that your career path is full of opportunities.

Where Did You Pick Up Your Attitude About Self Marketing?

In most cultures and most countries, parents raise their children to be humble, shy, and modest. One of parents' greatest fears is that their children will turn out to be braggarts. And no one likes a braggart. In the career workshops we conduct, we often ask our participants if their mothers ever sent them off to school with, *"Now you go to school and tell five people how wonderful you are today."* In the more than fifteen years we've been in business, not one person has answered *"yes."* More likely, you were raised with such sayings as:

- good work speaks for itself
- children should be seen and not heard

You bring such ideas to the marketplace. If you're not quite sure whether you're cut out for self marketing, you probably picked up on that attitude about self marketing from your parents and kept it for your own.

Consider the following: on an interview, who gets the offer—the best candidate or the best interviewee? The best interviewee, of course. The two may possibly be one and the same, but not necessarily. Whoever can talk about and present him or herself in the best manner will get the offer. When you're sitting in an interview, the interviewer is not going to consult with your mom, your teachers, your colleagues, or your former boss. It's strictly up to you to speak for yourself.

> *A company that was going through a major reorganization had to simultaneously lay off a large number of employees and redirect the others to new positions. Every department relinquished its employees, and the directors and vice presidents had to choose who would remain and what jobs they would hold. In a hotel room, the decision makers taped flip-chart pages listing all of the available positions around the perimeter of the room. Then, one by one, employees' names were called out and the directors had to answer "yes" or "no"—whether they wanted to keep that individual or not. One of the directors later told us about the process. "We were literally playing musical chairs with people's livelihoods. Unfortunately," he said, "a lot of people who were very good at what they did were let go simply because no one knew them. When their names were called, there was dead silence, and they were placed on the layoff list." Even the names of those who received a negative response were sometimes kept; a director who hadn't worked with them would opt to keep them, because at least they were known.*

Why Don't You Self Market?

If you have yet to attempt self marketing, there's probably a reason for it. We've identified five major reasons why people don't self market. All of our clients agree with at least four of the five.

"Marketing is an attitude, not a department."
Phil Wexler

Reason #1: You weren't raised that way

You had no messages early in life to market yourself. It's no wonder that we see a large number of adults, forty-plus-years-old, who go on an interview and can't bring themselves to market their skills and accomplishments. It's a shame.

We have had both men and women attend our workshops who were so uncomfortable with the idea of self marketing that they left the workshop at this point to go to the restroom. And they never came back. They were that uncomfortable with the idea of promoting their own worth.

Reason #2: You weren't taught how

In high school and college, your teachers filled your head with knowledge and concepts, but they neglected to show you how to use that knowledge to your advantage. Self-promotion skills are never taught. You may not be self marketing primarily because you never learned how. Well, stay tuned. We'll take care of that part.

Reason #3: You see poor examples at work

All organizations have employees who are better at self-promotion than they are at actually doing their jobs. We tend to view those people as negative role models for self marketing and steer away from them and self marketing itself. We say to ourselves: *"I am not like that. It's not me, and I'll never be that way."* To keep from getting caught, these people usually switch jobs or organizations frequently and/or they surround themselves with really good employees who do all the work *(behind-the-scenes),* while they get all the credit.

But self marketing isn't at all about playing golf, kissing up to the boss, and neglecting work. Poor examples shouldn't keep you from learning self-promotion skills that will help you advance in your career.

> *Michael Blake, a young engineer who had attended one of our workshops, told us that his first boss was a prime example of a reprehensible self marketer. "When I first started at the company, this boss brought me into his office," Michael said, "and told me, 'I spend 50 percent of my time promoting myself and making sure I'm on the right committee, 30 percent of my time looking for another job, and 20 percent actually working.' After he described his formula," Michael commented, "he told me that I was expected to do his work. I never, ever wanted to be like that. I thought self marketing was the worst thing in the world."*

Reason #4: You don't have time

Many of our clients have told us that they don't have time to self market. *"I can't do it,"* one young man said. *"My life is far too busy as it is. Self marketing would be too time-consuming."* Our response? *"If you get laid off, you'll have all the time in the world."* Even though you feel as if you don't have time, you need to make time.

If you do happen to get laid off, or if you decide to quit your current job, contacts won't suddenly appear. However, if you have already made the contacts and are nurturing them, you'll find the transition to a new job or career quicker and less stressful. So get out of your rut, dust off your rolodex, and don't have lunch with the same people every day.

Some of our clients own a small consulting firm; they realize that they have to self market. Otherwise, they'd be history. They have contracts in place a year ahead of time; and, to keep work coming in, they make time to publish and distribute brochures targeted at getting work for the following year.

Marketing Yourself and Your Career

> "Fears are learned, and if they are learned, then they can be unlearned."
> Karl Menninger

Reason #5: You fear rejection

If you don't ask, you don't have to hear *"no."* If you don't take a step out there, you don't have to hear *"no."* If you don't risk, you don't have to hear *"no."* It's comfortable to stay in your own cozy cubicle and not venture into self marketing.

The owners of the consulting firm we mentioned go on sixty interviews a year. Out of those sixty, how many jobs with contracts do you suppose they get? Fifty? Forty? No. The answer is twenty. That means they hear *"no"* forty times a year, or two-thirds of the time.

It's a numbers game. The only way you'll hear *"yes"* is if you hear *"no."* Getting ahead means putting yourself out there and seeing whether or not someone wants you. You have to get used to it, to learn to de-personalize the rejections. Self marketing involves getting over the fear of rejection.

Mary Connelly, an administrative assistant who attended one of our workshops, discovered that what kept her from self marketing was her upbringing, a lack of training, and a fear of rejection. Her company was going through a reorganization and gave Mary and other employees three months to find a new job. Mary decided to self market. She told us, "I knew that, in my circumstance, using the self-marketing skills I learned was a now-or-never proposition. I determined to make time to self market." Mary created a resume and distributed it internally with a letter to all of the people who had just gotten jobs as new department heads. "I let them know that I was available and would like to talk to them about becoming their administrative assistant." She was overwhelmed by the response to her letter. She generated a number of job interviews and landed a new position.

Doesn't It Sound Like Bragging?

You've read about the major reasons why people don't self market. Now it's time for a little quiz, a self assessment. Which reasons for not self marketing are ones that you have used, either consciously or subconsciously? Be honest. Once you've realized what has held you back, you'll be more ready to travel the road toward learning self marketing.

Why Haven't I Pursued the Self-Marketing Route?

Listed below are the different reasons for not self marketing. Following each is a continuum. Mark your place on the continuums by asking yourself, *"To what extent has each reason held me back from taking advantage of self marketing?"* One reflects little influence; five reflects maximum influence.

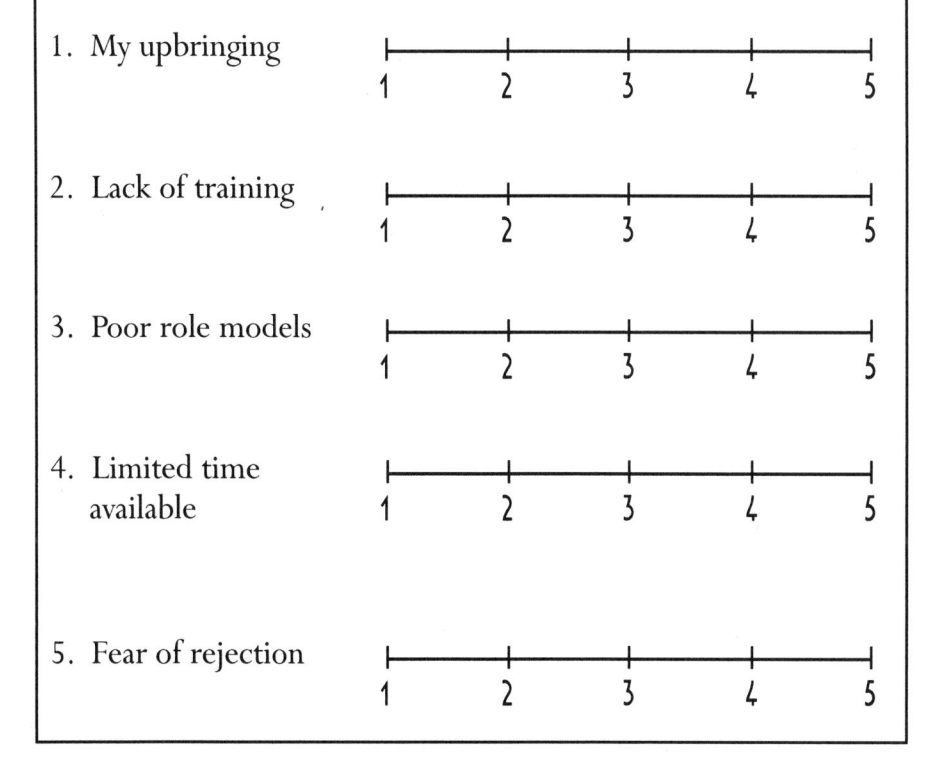

1. My upbringing
   1　2　3　4　5

2. Lack of training
   1　2　3　4　5

3. Poor role models
   1　2　3　4　5

4. Limited time available
   1　2　3　4　5

5. Fear of rejection
   1　2　3　4　5

Self Marketing Is the Way to Go

You may have gotten along fine without self marketing. Some people never promote their own skills and accomplishments and are quite satisfied with their present jobs or careers. We're not saying that you can't get along without it in some circumstances. It's very possible that you can. We just want you to know that self marketing can take you much further than you thought possible. It can open doors to new opportunities. And it just may help you land the job or career of your dreams.

However, to truly take advantage of self marketing, you have to do it continually. It must become a habit. Once you start to do it *(and we will show you comfortable ways to market yourself)*, it becomes ingrained.

Self-promotion skills are survival skills. You will be working for many different people, whether as an employee or as an independent contractor, throughout your working years. Knowing how to market yourself and your career will help you keep your head above water and keep you paddling even when you're in the midst of a career storm.

We want you to succeed. In our business of career consulting, we wouldn't have been able to keep the doors open if we hadn't helped our clients achieve success. That's why we tried everything until we found what worked. And that's what we want to share with you. We don't include resume writing or the steps involved in a successful interview, because those topics have been written about time and time again. We want to provide you with tips and secrets and common sense advice that you can really use. We want you to read this book, apply it to your career, and say, *"Yes! It really works!"*

> "If you don't promote yourself—a terrible thing happens—nothing."
> Anonymous

What can self marketing do for you? It will provide you with:

- the freedom to move when and where you want to *(you don't need to stay in a job that you don't like because you don't know how to find a new one)*

- confidence and control *(people who feel stuck often get angry; people who know how to promote their own accomplishments and skills have confidence that they can choose their own destiny)*

- more interesting work *(self marketing enables you to negotiate for work that fits your preferred skills)*

- pay that reflects your worth *(when you know what you have to offer and can verbalize your worth, you can negotiate for pay that reflects it)*

It's in your best interest to learn how to promote yourself. Get over the notion that your good work and good deeds will speak for themselves. When our clients tell us that, we ask, *"And when did your good work grow lips?"* You, and you alone, are responsible for letting others in the world of work know what you can do. Take advantage of this opportunity to learn how to do it well.

Summary

There's no better time than the present for learning how to promote your skills and accomplishments. Even if you've been wary of self marketing in the past, whether it's been due to your upbringing, lack of training, poor examples, lack of time, and/or fear of rejection, you can make the decision to acquire self-marketing skills. They'll give you the confidence and freedom to move ahead in your career. It does take commitment, but once you learn how to self market, it will become a habit that you'll never want to break.

Chapter 2 Key Points

- 🗝 Marketing is not just selling; it's a mix of the five P's—product, promotion, place, price, and positioning

- 🗝 Likewise, self marketing is more than just preparing your resume in hopes of selling yourself; it also involves the five P's

- 🗝 All the ingredients in your self-marketing mix need to be present and in correct proportion to one another

Making Sense of the Marketing Mix

2

When we lead workshops in self marketing, we ask participants, *"When you hear the term 'marketing,' what comes to mind?"* and their first response is always *"Selling."* But the two aren't interchangeable. Selling yourself is only a small segment of the whole self-marketing process. That's why we talk about the marketing process in general, because it sheds light on the self-promotion process.

What Is Marketing Anyway?

In the absence of good marketing, most people rely on selling alone, because they don't know any other way to go about it. Marketing is much, much more than that. It's a whole formula, a strategy companies use to sell their products. In traditional terms, it's referred to as the *"marketing mix,"* a pot of ingredients critical to successful sales. Used correctly, the marketing mix translates into a recipe for success.

What's part of the marketing mix? Identified as the five P's, product, price, promotion, place, and positioning, all play prominent parts in the marketing strategy.

Product

A company's *"product strategy"* refers to its package or assortment of products or services. It includes what is being sold, the quality level, the number and type of items to sell, packaging, features and related service, and when to drop existing offerings. Some products/services a company wishes to market may be complementary to each other *(hammers and nails)* or might be substitutes for each other *(butter or margarine)*.

Promotion

Promotion refers to all of a company's communication efforts, both direct and indirect, in support of the sale of the product. It is often categorized into *"push"* and *"pull"* approaches. The *"push"* approach includes efforts to stimulate sales through promotional efforts with distributors and others in the distribution channel, while the *"pull"* approach focuses on promotion to the end buyer, to stimulate demand and pull in customers. Promotion decisions include the selection of *"tools"* (*i.e., advertising, press releases, publicity, personal selling, point-of-purchase displays, and sales promotions*).

Place

The place element of the marketing mix refers to the strategy and tactics employed to make the product available to buyers. A company must decide whether to handle its own retailing or sell to retailers or wholesalers, what type and number of outlets are appropriate, and what type of distribution pattern will work best—

> *"Show people what they want most, and they will move heaven and earth to get it."*
> Frank Bettger

selective, extensive, targeting geographical areas only, etc. For example, WalMart was targeted for places where the other competitors weren't—in small towns and out-of-the-way places.

Price

A company determines price in view of competition, market expectations, quality perceptions, alternative product offerings, market share, profitability goals, and various other factors. Pricing decisions include determining the overall level of prices, the range of prices, the relationship between price and quality, and the extent to which price plays a role in the promotion process.

Positioning

The fifth P, positioning, is the sum total of all of the company's marketing efforts, as reflected in the market's perception of the company. Positioning includes emphasizing such attributes as the price leader, the quality leader, the service leader, the family-oriented company, the innovator, etc.

For example, in the car industry, the way different manufacturers position themselves reflects their marketing mix. Volvo appeals to those who desire safety and BMW appeals to the status seekers. Hotels do the same. Look at the following continuum and see where the different hotels are placed, from a Motel 6 to a Ritz Carlton.

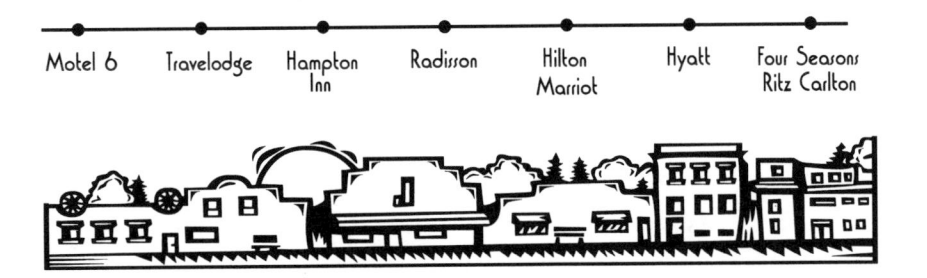

> "There is no such thing as 'soft sell' and 'hard sell.' There is only 'smart sell' and 'stupid sell.'"
> Charles Brower

| Motel 6 | Travelodge | Hampton Inn | Radisson | Hilton Marriot | Hyatt | Four Seasons Ritz Carlton |

A Motel 6 appeals to a different group of people than a Ritz Carlton or a Marriott does. Each has been marketed carefully to reflect its specific mix. The product *(the hotel and the services offered)* looks different, the price varies, locations differ, and the promotional strategy depends on the positioning of the hotel on the continuum.

If the marketing mix is not properly maintained or is changed without regard to all of the P's, sales slip. A Travelodge can't up its price significantly in hopes of positioning itself differently without also changing the other P's in the mix. Customers just won't buy it.

How Does the Marketing Mix Relate to Your Career Development?

Trying to sell yourself without considering all the factors involved in self marketing is like a company trying to sell a tube of toothpaste without any regard to quality, special features, pricing of competitive tubes, advertising and publicity concerns, or how and where to place the toothpaste. Success is in the positioning.

Positioning

How will your mix come together? Will you:

- take the time to know yourself well enough to promote yourself effectively?
- consider what message you're trying to send, and how and to whom it will be sent?
- decipher who will be the purchaser of your skills and compete in that market?
- price yourself in regards to your message, your skills, and where you want to work?

Self marketing is an extension of marketing itself. Putting together a marketing package and positioning yourself will enable you to self market effectively, without the frustration we see and hear from so many clients who have no idea how to go about the whole self-marketing process. In this book, we'll teach you how to identify and create your own marketing mix.

> "Life consists not in holding good cards, but in playing those you do hold well."
> Josh Billings

Product

Believe it or not, many of our clients believe that the product they present is their resume. It's not just that. In self marketing, the product refers to your skills, accomplishments, degrees, credentials, training, background, experience, job titles, personality, image, and attitudes.

The strategy you need to devise depends on the message you want to promote. Which of your features are most important in your current or hoped-for career? You may not even be aware of all your skills or even what you want out of a job or career. If that's the case, you may wish to read *Unlocking Your Career Potential*. It puts you in touch with your desires, skills, and needs. In this book—*Marketing Yourself and Your Career*—we'll help you document your successes in specific terms.

Promotion

To promote yourself in the best manner, you'll need to focus in on the message you're sending to decide how it will be sent and to whom you're going to send it. You may choose to self market both formally and informally, to your boss and colleagues, or to the decision makers at a totally different company. You'll need to do some advance planning and create a self-marketing script that highlights your best features. Knowing how and to whom you intend to promote yourself saves unnecessary time going about the process in the wrong way.

Marketing Yourself and Your Career

> "The man on the top of the mountain didn't fall there."
> Anonymous

Place

How will you make yourself available to those you want to purchase your skills—the end buyers? Will you try to set up an interview with someone at each company or someone in each department of your organization that you're interested in? If you want to self market successfully, you'll need to determine the places where you will self market. You'll have to identify places in both your professional life **and** your personal life, from the cafeteria at work to your orthodontist's waiting room. And you will have to get comfortable with the fact that self marketing has to take place continually if you want to make headway.

Price

As a self marketer, you have to price yourself according to the message you're sending, the product you're delivering, the market you're attempting to enter, etc. It has to match the rest of your marketing mix. If you price yourself too high, you might not be bought. If you price yourself too low, your potential employer may be suspicious that your product isn't good enough; besides, it may take you years to get caught up to the market price.

> *One of our client organizations ran an ad in the newspaper for a shipping clerk. The range in experience and prices was wide. A number of applicants marketed themselves incorrectly for the position. Some applicants were engineers and revealed no match between their experience and what skills were needed for the position. Three applicants showed up at the door on the Monday after the ad was run. "They showed initiative," Mark, the personnel director, told us, "but they weren't qualified for the position. They merely wasted their time." The applicants that were qualified asked for hourly rates that varied from six to twelve dollars an hour. "We settled on one young man that asked for nine dollars an hour. But we considered the twelve-dollar applicant and would have paid him that had he promoted himself more eagerly."*

Take the following self-assessment to determine if your self-marketing efforts have been working.

How Well Is My Marketing Mix Working?

To what extent do you agree that your self-marketing strategies and techniques have been working? Place yourself on each of the continuums that follow. A check mark near the one means *"I don't agree at all"*; a check mark near the five means *"I enthusiastically agree."*

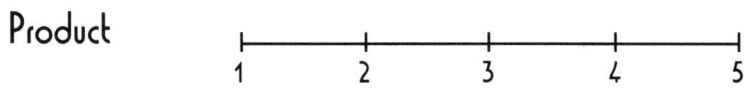

Product

|—1—|—2—|—3—|—4—|—5—|

I know myself, have determined my features, and have packaged myself well.

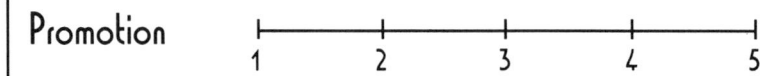

Promotion

|—1—|—2—|—3—|—4—|—5—|

I've honed the message I'm sending and have determined how it will be sent and who will help me get the message across.

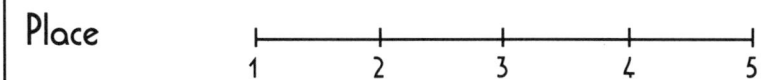

Place

|—1—|—2—|—3—|—4—|—5—|

I am marketing myself continually, both formally and informally, to people at work and to people I have just met.

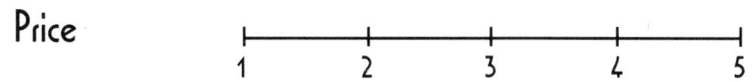

Price

|—1—|—2—|—3—|—4—|—5—|

I have priced myself according to my total package and to the market I'm attempting to enter.

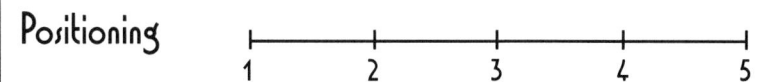

Positioning

|—1—|—2—|—3—|—4—|—5—|

I have positioned myself so that prospective or current employers know exactly what I have to offer and why I have priced myself as I have.

Scoring Key

If you marked all or most of the five P's with a 3 or less, then you have some work ahead of you. But don't despair. Read through this book from cover to cover and practice your self-marketing skills until they become second nature.

If you marked all or most of the five P's with a 4 or a 5, congratulations! You've done great on marketing yourself in your current position. However, if you're headed somewhere else, you'll do well to polish your skills by reading through each chapter and determining where you need extra practice.

Do you fall somewhere in between? Self-marketing skills will always benefit you, so be sure you've mastered all of them in order to cook up the marketing mix that's right for you.

Corrina Smythe, a client of ours with an MBA in marketing, knew she had to start looking for another job when her company informed her that they were downsizing. We taught Corrina about self marketing and let her in on the ingredients in the marketing mix. She immediately saw the connection between self marketing and finding a good job of her choice. Corrina was very aware of her product (herself) and long before she had to leave, she promoted herself to individuals at different companies within the same industry. She thought about where she'd like to work and researched how she should price herself. Her positioning was strong. Corrina marketed herself to a competitor and was hired. She also negotiated a $35,000 sign-on bonus. "Self marketing made all the difference," she told us.

Making Sense of the Marketing Mix

Self marketing only comes together when you have the right mix. Few people realize this. When we tell participants in our workshops that self marketing involves a combination of different ingredients, they're often surprised. *"But knowing the recipe and mixing the ingredients in the right amounts makes the difference between a self marketer who doesn't get what he wants and a self promoter who hits his target,"* we say. You have to know what it takes. Stick with us while we reveal the nitty-gritty details of what you need to do.

Summary

Knowing the ingredients involved in the marketing mix gives you an edge in learning how to self market. Self marketing is more than just a sales tactic. It involves knowing yourself and what you bring to the table, being able to promote your message to the right people in the right places, pricing yourself correctly, and positioning yourself for the greatest impact on your career. It's a tried-and-true method. You just have to use it.

Chapter 3 Key Points

- ⚷ Creating your product package involves documenting your skills and accomplishments, and choosing which features and benefits you want to highlight

- ⚷ Putting together an *"I love me"* file will give you a head start in self marketing and will make it easier for you to write bullet statements

- ⚷ Bullet statements reveal the features and benefits of your product package; they describe what you've done and what happened as a result

- ⚷ If you're serious about self marketing, you should use bullet statements on a daily basis, in both formal and informal situations

- ⚷ Pricing yourself correctly involves labor market research; additionally, your price must match the other ingredients of your marketing mix

Jump-Starting the Self-Marketing Process

3

In self marketing, the emphasis is on *you*. You are the product that needs to be packaged and sold, so you'll be working on how best to do that. Yes, eventually you will need to get out there and sell yourself; but, in order to do that successfully, you'll have to know yourself, your skills, and your accomplishments inside-out, and you'll have to price yourself accordingly. For some of our clients, this part of the process is fairly simple and enjoyable; for others, it's like pulling teeth.

Why Create a "Product" Package

You are a composite of many skills, various accomplishments, and a wide range of experiences. So how do you let your current boss or prospective employer in on everything you are and can do? By packaging yourself so that your *"customers"* know what they are

Marketing Yourself and Your Career

buying *(e.g., when you're applying for a position)* or what they've bought *(e.g., when negotiating for a raise or a promotion)*. The more effectively you package yourself, the more clearly your customers can see whether they want or will pay more for what you have to offer.

> *A participant in one of our workshops took offense at the whole idea of packaging herself. In the midst of a discussion on the topic, she raised her hand and said, "I'm sorry, but I have a problem with this." "Really?" we asked her. "What seems to be the problem?" "Well," she began, "I've never viewed myself as a product, and packaging just seems dishonest. It seems like I'd be pushing the issue too far." She didn't understand the benefits of marketing until we explained to her that all the perfume out there does the same thing. "You are buying the box and the bottle," we said. "And if you don't have a box and a bottle, an interviewer won't see how you stand out from the rest."*

Whenever you present yourself formally *(e.g., in a job interview)* or informally *(e.g., in everyday conversation)*, you need to focus on the specifics of what you can do or what you've done. Most people talk in glittering generalities, such as:

- *"I'm good"*
- *"I'm great with people"*
- *"I'm a hard worker"*
- *"I've got a degree in (fill in the blank)"*

"Every prospect listens to his or her own inner radio, WII-FM—What's In It For Me?"
William T. Brooks

So what? Those phrases are not terrific self-marketing tools. Until you start to document your skills and accomplishments in the form of bullet statements *(we'll show you how soon)*, you're never going to impress anybody, get the job or promotion you want, or earn the money you think you deserve. Generalities make you sound like everybody else. They're flat, unimpressive, and ho-hum.

Bullet statements focus on what you've done and what you can do for others. Writing bullet statements means that you have to look back on the events of your life and pull meaningful accomplishments from them, accomplishments that market you successfully. Bullet statements reveal the features and benefits of your product package; they succinctly describe the accomplishments and skills that you want to stand out.

> "Life, like a mirror, never gives back more than we put into it."
> Anonymous

The owners of a small consulting firm liked the idea of bullet statements so much, they incorporated them into their Monday morning meetings. Ernie Maxwell, one of the owners, explained their process to us. "We went around the room every week and had our employees tell us a bullet statement about what they had accomplished the previous week." "How did it work?" we asked. "At the beginning," Ernie explained, "our employees gnashed their teeth and hated it. In fact, the first time we did it, one young woman said, 'I didn't do anything last week.' I said, 'That's great. Give me back your paycheck. Why should I pay you if you didn't do anything?'" Ernie went on to say that things improved rapidly after that point. "Employees got so used to sharing their bullet statements that they looked forward to Monday morning meetings, because they enjoyed telling what they did and had fun hearing other people's stories. When we had to downsize, the employees who left had no trouble at all writing their resumes."

Putting Together an "I Love Me" File

To write effective bullet statements, you must remember your skills and accomplishments. However, the older you are and the more jobs you have held, the more difficult it is for you to remember all of them. That's why we ask our clients to create an *"I love me"* file. What is an *"I love me"* file, you ask? It's similar to the file of report cards, awards, and mementos your parents kept for you or which you are creating for your children. The *"I love me"* file is just an adult version.

What goes in your *"I love me"* file? So many different items that we suggest you clean your desk, clear out your closets, and go on a data search. You'll be looking for:

- copies of your resumes or job applications *(include **all** resumes, because different resumes will highlight different skills and accomplishments)*

- all old performance evaluations *(if you don't have them, your old employers will; you may have to pay for a copy, but it's worth it)*

- any letters of recommendation

- anything written about you *(were you written up in a company newsletter, featured in a volunteer newsletter, a magazine review, etc.?)*

- any awards or certificates you received, for either professional or volunteer work

- samples of your work

- letters from satisfied customers, students, trainees, etc.

- your bullet statements written on 3x5 cards *(every time you've had a major accomplishment that can be written as a bullet statement, do so and place in your file)*

You need to have a hard copy of all the items in your file. So if you have some of the items on disk or on the hard drive of your computer, make a copy and drop it in your file.

Without an *"I love me"* file, you'll fall prey to what many of our clients do—forgetitis. Without data to back up what you've accomplished in your lifetime, you'll forget it. If you have the information at your fingertips, you'll find it so much easier to write a new resume or list your skills or create bullet statements to help you get that new job, promotion, or raise. If you only write bullet statements every ten years, you'll leave out more than what you'll include. So use the information in your *"I love me"* file to spark your memory. When you get ready to formally market yourself, you won't have to take a long walk down memory lane.

Your *"I love me"* file is invaluable. And you only have to update it once or twice a year. It's actually a great morale booster, and you can take it with you on an internal or external interview. It is by no means used on every interview, but should someone want a sample of something, it's worth a thousand words. It's your success portfolio.

> "Don't tell me how hard you work. Tell me how much you get done."
> James Ling

Hitting Your Target with Bullet Statements

You'll need the information in your *"I love me"* file to help you write bullet statements, and you'll place your statements back in your file when you've finished writing them. So what exactly are bullet statements? They are action- and result-oriented statements that tell your listeners what you have done and what you're going to do for them, in very specific terms. In marketing lingo, they're referred to as benefit statements. We like to call them bullet statements, because they're aimed at hitting a target—your contacts, your boss, or a prospective employer.

Marketing Yourself and Your Career

The process you will go through in order to write bullet statements—the sitting down and looking at your life to document your successes and accomplishments *(many should be found in your "I love me" file)*—gives you confidence that you have the skills and abilities to do what you're about to do, whether that means finding a new job, asking for a promotion, or negotiating a raise.

We've had many, many clients who, after they discover they want to change careers or take on new responsibilities at work, balk at doing it. *"I can't do this,"* they've told us. *"I really don't think I can handle it."* But when they take the time to go back through their work histories *(paid and unpaid)*, they realize that they do have the necessary skills for the work they'd like to do. Documenting successes and writing them in bullet statements gives you the courage to work at something new, different, or at a higher level.

What will bullet statements help you do?

Bullet statements are such short, action-oriented statements, that they deter people from talking ad nauseam about themselves. If you're at the water cooler with a manager from another department or in a job interview with the personnel director from another company, you don't want to dawdle. You must get your point across quickly. What you don't want to do is relate a long, drawn-out story about what you did and how you did it, because by the time you finish, your audience isn't even sure why you started the story in the first place. Bullet statements are fast and sharp, and they hit their target.

We can't tell you how many interviewers say they appreciate people who know what they can do and who can quickly tell you what they've done. One interviewer told us about a young man he was interviewing for a managerial position. The man seemed quite capable, but he rambled on and on about his experiences, never

> "Whatever you can do, or dream you can, begin it. Boldness has genius, power, and magic in it. Begin it now."
> Goethe

connecting those experiences with the managerial position he was after. He didn't get the job.

Interviewers, bosses, and contact people want to know two things, and two things only: what you did and what happened as a result. If you want to list your tasks and responsibilities on your resume or recite them to current or prospective employers, you'd better be prepared to tell what resulted from those tasks and responsibilities. Too many people leave it at: *"I was responsible for the annual awards banquet."* Well? Did you have it? Did anyone come? And, if people did attend, what happened while they were there?

Going through the process of writing bullet statements allows you to think about your work successes, to be succinct, and to give a coherent answer that anyone could understand. And that's important, because successful self marketing means that you'll be sharing your bullet statements continually—with a friend over lunch in the company cafeteria, in a job interview, or with a new contact at your kid's soccer game.

> "The best way to sell yourself is to make it easy to buy."
> Anonymous

In our workshops, we teach people how to write effective bullet statements by coaching them to continually ask "So what?" after any general statement they make. We get them going by having them analyze statements we make about what we've done. Some of our work deals with training groups of people within corporations that are downsizing. So we start by giving a general process statement: "We've held forty training sessions, each eight hours long, over two months, and we've passed out one million pieces of paper." Our audience shouts back, "SO WHAT?" Next, we fall back on a glittering generality, and say, "Well, everybody was really motivated when they left. They liked it a lot, and they laughed." Again, the audience shouts back, "SO WHAT?" Finally, we get to the heart of the matter and state, "In outplacement training, we usually reduce the number of lawsuits against the organization. There have been only two lawsuits out of one thousand employees, and the expectation was that there would be at least ten or fifteen."

Marketing Yourself and Your Career

> "We don't see things as they are; we see things as we are."
> — Anais Nin

Bullet statements allow people to own what they do, something they may never have done in the past. If you are part of a team working on a large project, you need to preface your bullet statements with, *"As a member of a team, I..."* People are afraid of taking too much credit, but they still need to recognize their part in a team or group's success.

Part of the magic of writing bullet statements is that it allows you to see patterns and themes in your skills or accomplishments. After writing ten or twelve, you won't need to write any more, because you'll end up repeating yourself. The other part of the magic is what happens when you take a pen and start writing about yourself and your successes. You don't write about things you don't want to do. If you dislike generating reports, even if you are good at it, you won't write a bullet statement about it. You'll have erased it from your repertoire of successes. You automatically start writing about things you like and have enjoyed doing. It gets you in tune with your preferred skills.

Learning to write bullet statements

To write effective bullet statements, you will need information, but you may not always have all the data you need in your *"I love me"* file. Many people neglect to find out exactly how their work has benefited their previous employers, especially in statistical terms. Did you increase sales, and by how much? Did your work streamline a process and result in savings of both time and money? If yes, how great were those savings? Part of the reason why employees don't know this information is because employers are lax about letting their workers know how they fit into the big picture. But it's this type of information you need for your bullet statements.

Jump-Starting the Self-Marketing Process

If you can contact former bosses or colleagues, by all means do so. However, if you can't get hold of the data you need or the results have never been tabulated, don't make it up. You may get caught. If you don't know how much something increased, don't say it increased by thirty or fifty percent. Your interviewer might ask you how you know, and you'll be at a loss for words. Just say it increased.

What people get hung up on when writing bullet statements is that not everything they do has a measurable result. Not everything results in increased percentages or profits, but everything has an ending. The way to get around this is to ask yourself after you've written what you've done: *"So what?"* or *"What happened?"* or *"What would have happened if I had not done this?"* It makes you focus on the importance of your task.

> *One of our clients, Ally Schneider, had trouble coming up with bullet statements. She was a marketing assistant whose husband was being transferred out of state, so she needed to find a new position. We asked her to document her successes, and she was at a loss. "This process won't work for me," Ally told us. "I've only done what people have told me to do. I don't have any successes to share." "Sure, you do, Ally," we told her, and before long she came up with, "I set up fifty speaking engagements in six months." "Okay," we responded, "but so what?" Ally thought. "My boss spoke fifty times in six months." "Yes," we said again, "but so what? What happened as a result of those fifty speaking engagements?" She didn't know, so we told her to go ask her boss. Ally did so, and came back with, "As a result of those fifty speaking engagements, my boss got 125 new clients and increased his sales by $200,000." Ally was on her way to writing effective bullet statements.*

Writing bullet statements is often trickier than it looks. We've found that our clients are most successful when they see how other people have written them and then practice writing bullet statements themselves. The following bullet statements should stimulate your thinking. Many of them are transferable to at least ten different careers or jobs.

1. Reduced costs and overhead expenses by careful monitoring and control of financial assistance and repayment procedures.

2. Conducted fifteen-hour training course for newly-recruited volunteers; increased effectiveness by 50 percent.

3. Founded a real estate partnership while in law school. Parlayed the original investment capital of $30,000 into over $500,000 in five years.

4. Was instrumental in founding the University of San Diego Business Association. Developed a program to create an awareness of and an interest in the business community.

5. Directed a team of eight professionals to assess needs, establish goals, and target objectives to meet the individual needs of a group of handicapped individuals.

6. Installed a complete accounting system, by department, in a large agency; decreased operation cost by 25 percent.

7. Conceived a new management-information service procedure that made vital operation reports available to management the following day.

8. Discovered technical and marketing problems in a planned new product area and prevented a potential loss of more than $100,000.

9. Formulated policies and procedures for the administration of zoning petitions resulting in the reduction of processing time by nearly 25 percent.

10. Prevented a potentially volatile ethnic incident from erupting in a racially-sensitive community by initiating supervised neighborhood talk-groups.

11. Developed and installed a unique laboratory organization that eliminated duplication and encouraged cooperation. Reduced costs by $100,000.

12. Initiated and directed a Community Services Program that incorporated a complete training program for future public administrators and processed every citizen complaint or request.

13. Significantly reduced friction among four major departments through a series of problem-solving seminars.

14. Organized and trained a sales force for selected marketing territories that resulted in a 67 percent increase in sales and profits.

15. Initiated a volunteer fund-raising campaign that brought in $150,000 more in contributions than all previous directors brought in.

16. As a part-time sales employee, I sold over $5,000 of merchandise during Christmas vacation. I was cited by my supervisor for outstanding performance.

17. Significantly contributed to the writing of new curriculum manuals for high school English. Broadened the scope of interest to students, resulting in a diminished truancy statistic.

18. Remodeled and redecorated our home, which was then chosen for inclusion in the city's Tour of Beautiful Homes to benefit the city's restoration fund.

19. Served as a project manager for several major research programs involving hundreds of thousands of dollars in grants and government allocations. Projects were completed on time and within budget.

20. Set up weekly luncheon fashion shows for major hotel chain. Increased luncheon attendance and provided excellent exposure for designers, vendors, and the store involved.

> "The greatest thing in this world is not so much where we are, but in what direction we are moving."
> Oliver Wendell Holmes

Marketing Yourself and Your Career

Are you getting a better idea of what a bullet statement is? The people who wrote the preceding bullet statements identified a situation, the action they took, and the results they achieved. Once you've come up with these three categories, your bullet statements will be easier to write.

First, you'll list the SITUATION. You'll need to state the situation or problem that confronted you. Try to be as detailed and specific as possible.

Second, you'll describe the ACTION you took. You will have to recall what you did to solve the problem. Use an action verb, or more than one action verb, if appropriate.

Third, you'll report the RESULTS. Your objective is to tell what the outcome was of the action you took. Quantify, if possible, and use percentages and estimates.

You'll be writing your bullet statements in two drafts. The first draft will contain jargon and work content. As you write the second draft, be conscious of words that aren't transferable. For example, use *"organization"* instead of *"school,"* and use *"client"* or *"participant"* instead of *"student"* or *"patient."*

Finally, when you've finished your second draft of Situation-Action-Results, you will formulate a short, concise statement that communicates your skill. This will be your final bullet statement, and you should be able to use it in any conversation.

Follow along as we take you through the process of writing bullet statements for communication, interpersonal, and technical skills. Then we'll give you a chance to try your hand at writing them.

"If you cannot do great things, do small things in a great way."
J. F. Clarke

Communication Skills

Situation:	I needed to write the marketing plan for the largest market in our company.
Action:	Gathered objectives and plans from each area, compiled, and then wrote my own section.
Results:	All marketing department personnel were clear on goals, and management had one document to track the objectives through the year.
Bullet Statement:	Gathered and compiled objectives and plans from each department to create a marketing plan for the Los Angeles/Orange area. All marketing department personnel were clear on goals, and management had one document to track the objectives through the year.

Situation:	I needed to write a comprehensive description of all financial services offered by Coast Savings and Loan.
Action:	I gathered all the information available from other departments and organized it.
Results:	Tellers and new-accounts people had one place to go for all account information. Additionally, marketing/advertising had a consistent reference for copywriting.
Bullet Statement:	Wrote a comprehensive description of all the financial services offered by Coast Savings and Loan. The reference book gave the tellers and new-accounts people one place to go for information, and it provided consistent information for the marketing and advertising department.

Marketing Yourself and Your Career

Situation:	I needed to inform local residents about an Easter Sunrise Service at Marineland.
Action:	Wrote a press release and had duplicates of a photo from a previous year's service made. Pulled the mailing lists from media source books. Handled all aspects of the mailing.
Results:	Several papers picked up on the story. There was standing room only at Marineland's Dolphin Arena. Two hundred to three hundred more participants than the previous year attended.
Bullet Statement:	Publicized an Easter Sunrise Service at Marineland through press releases and direct mail. The event was standing room only and had 300 more attendees than last year.

Interpersonal Skills

Situation:	I was the liaison between my company and our advertising agency.
Action:	I established rapport with the ad agency.
Results:	We had good morale and a free flow of information between agency and company.
Bullet Statement:	Acted as liaison between my company and our advertising agency. Established a rapport with agency personnel and encouraged a free flow of information.

Jump-Starting the Self-Marketing

Situation:	PacTel Cellular needed a marketing representative to represent Cellular at the Pacific Telesis quarterly roundtable meetings.
Action:	I attended the quarterly meetings, bringing PacTel Cellular's opinion to the meetings and bringing back Telesis activities to the company.
Results:	Telesis advertising/marketing managers consistently called me instead of the heads of the departments, because they had come to trust me and my ability to get the information they needed.
Bullet Statement:	Acted as a marketing representative to represent my company at the Pacific Telesis quarterly roundtable meetings. Telesis advertising/marketing managers consistently called me instead of other heads of departments, because they had come to trust me and my ability to get the information they needed.

Technical Skills

Situation:	Needed to keep track of our household budget.
Action:	Purchased a MacIntosh SE with Excel software. Developed a program to track all checks and deposits.
Results:	Closer track of expenses and the ability to locate unplanned expenses better.
Bullet Statement:	Purchased a MacIntosh SE with Excel software and developed a program that tracked all checks and deposits in order to monitor our household expenses and locate unplanned expenses.

Your Career

Feeling a bit more confident about writing bullet statements? Why don't you try your hand at writing two? We'll provide the Situation-Action-Results, and you write the bullet statements.

Situation:	I needed to track lead expenses to advertising costs.
Action:	I developed a spreadsheet on Lotus 1-2-3 and later moved it to Microsoft Excel. The spreadsheet allowed me to track expenses as well as do analyses of various media selections.
Results:	Lower cost per lead once tracking began. Ability to provide upper management daily/weekly/monthly/ quarterly summaries of activity.
Bullet Statement:	_____ _____ _____ _____

Situation:	I was the first person at PacTel to hold my position (I joined the company when it was a "start-up" company).
Action:	I developed all the filing systems and procedures, and structured the department.
Results:	Department grew from one person to five in three years.
Bullet Statement:	_____ _____ _____ _____

Now it's time for you to write two of your own Situation-Action-Results and their corresponding bullet statements.

Bullet Statements

Situation: _____
_____
_____
_____

Action: _____
_____
_____
_____

Results: _____
_____
_____
_____

Bullet Statement: _____
_____
_____
_____

Marketing Yourself and Your Career

Bullet Statements

Situation: _____
_____
_____
_____

Action: _____
_____
_____
_____

Results: _____
_____
_____
_____

Bullet Statement: _____
_____
_____
_____

Using Your Product Knowledge

Bullet statements can be used in a number of ways. They can be used in informal settings, such as:

- when talking to colleagues
- in professional meetings with your peers
- when conversing with your boss at the company picnic
- in the midst of a training class

Bob, a client of ours in the middle of his MBA program, related a work accomplishment in the form of a bullet statement to his group during a class break. A woman in his group heard Bob's statement and said to herself, *"We need someone to do that in our company."* She helped Bob get an interview and eventually land a job in her company.

> *Monica Breyer, a participant in one of our workshops, called to tell us how she had received a job offer by self marketing in an informal setting. A special education teacher for the deaf and mentally handicapped, Monica, through our program, had identified that she wanted to be in training. While flying to a family emergency, she happened to strike up a conversation with her seat partner. "He asked me what I did, and I was prepared to answer, thanks to your training," she told us. "I am a teacher and a trainer. I love to take complicated ideas and break them down into smaller parts. I take them to my students' level of learning and am thrilled when they grasp the previously unattainable concepts." Monica's seat partner was the owner of a national hamburger chain. He was extremely dissatisfied with his trainers, whom he thought trained too theoretically. He made Monica a job offer on the spot.*

"Your most important sale in life is to sell yourself to yourself."
Maxwell Maltz

Bullet statements are also used in formal settings. They're used:

- in resumes
- in cover letters
- on job applications
- during job interviews
- during performance evaluations

Of all the formal settings for using bullet statements, performance evaluations are rarely, if ever, considered when thinking of places to self market. Too many employees approach performance evaluations in a *"sit-and-listen"* fashion and do no preparation whatsoever. But the purpose of a good performance evaluation is not only for you to receive feedback about your skills and abilities; it also provides a great opportunity for you to tell your employer what you've accomplished during the past year, especially if you want a raise, a promotion, or a different job.

Most employees aren't aware of this. We usually broach the topic with participants in our workshops by saying, *"Let's assume that you have accomplished ten major things in the past year. How many of those things do you think your boss knows about?"* We hear answers that range anywhere from 40 to 80 percent.

But the real answer is that bosses are aware of approximately 20 percent of what their employees have accomplished. Why? Because they're busy managing many other people, and they're busy managing their own careers. They cannot possibly know what you do every minute of the day, and you can't expect them to.

That is why it is absolutely critical that you prepare for your performance evaluation. To prepare adequately, sit down and write ten bullet statements about what you've achieved during the past year. When your boss is finished giving you feedback, you then say, *"Now I'd like to tell you what I've accomplished during the year,"* and you present your bullet statements. If you have a request after that—

"Luck is what happens when preparation meets opportunity."
Elmer Letterman

a raise, a promotion, or a different job—your boss will be much more willing to listen to you, because he or she can see why you should get your request.

> *Felicia, a client of ours, approached her boss, a dentist, for a raise. She told him her rent went up. Well, Felicia didn't get the raise. She told us her story, and we helped her see what she should have done. Felicia could have—and should have—documented that she had brought in new patients, made patients comfortable, conducted inventory assessments, and ordered supplies from a different vendor to save money. Felicia needed to give a bottom-line reason for her request. It's vital that you do the same.*

You don't automatically get a raise just because you're a year older. As a year older, you only cost your organization more money. Insurance premiums increase, new taxes add a burden, and stock options based on your salary get more costly. You need to prove your worth. You must continually ask yourself, *"What have I done for my organization lately?"*

Setting the Right Price for Yourself

Once you've created and packaged your product, you need to put a price on it. And, believe us, price can be of paramount importance when you're applying for a job or asking for a raise. Price yourself too high and you'll get neither. Too low, and if you do get the job or raise, you'll be depressed when you finally realize how you shortchanged yourself.

How do you go about determining the right price? Start by asking people in your own organization about different salaries for different level jobs. Now, this may be a bit tricky. First, organizations don't necessarily want you to know what other people are making. And second, some people don't care to share such information.

So, if you're attempting to price different positions in your organization, approach employees informally and don't ask for their specific salaries. Say something like, *"If I were to get some training so that I could work in your department, what type of salary range would I be looking at?"* At least you won't be guessing in the dark.

Additionally, to determine salary ranges for your particular job or the job you would like to have:

- read the want ads in the newspaper
- subscribe to professional journals *(they also have ads in them)*
- attend professional meetings *(you can also uncover salary ranges for similar jobs in different industries; for example, if you're after a job in training and development, you may find that in one industry it pays $85,000 a year, and in another industry, it pays $45,000)*

Professional organizations typically perform salary surveys every year, so check out the results if the position you're in or the job you're after is under the umbrella of a professional organization. You'll see the salary ranges for different industries and different geographical locations. Then you can price yourself according to your skills, your training, your experience, and the type and location of industry you either do or would like to work in.

> *One of our clients, Bonnie Salsito, a teacher, had identified through our career development process that she wanted be in training and development. She had taught adults in night school and enjoyed it. Bonnie joined and volunteered for the American Society for Training and Development and conducted salary surveys within that organization. In the ASTD newsletter, when Bonnie found a job opening with a major mortuary, she knew it was a high-paying industry*

> *because of the research she had done. Typically, the starting salary for a position in training and development would be $45,000-$50,000. But Bonnie's research revealed that a mortuary would pay closer to $60,000. Because she had done her homework, she packaged herself at $60,000 and got the job.*

Match your price to what you've accomplished and what you have to offer. Remember, it should reflect the rest of your marketing mix. If you're a great product, are marketing yourself in a high-level organization, and have promoted yourself well, you can set a high price, because you're positioned at the top. On the other hand, if you've got decent potential but little experience, are marketing yourself in the non-profit sector, and have done minimal promotion, you might position yourself at the lower end of the price range and set a goal to move higher each year. Your marketing mix has to make sense.

Summary

You have to begin your self-marketing process with a good look at yourself and what you can do. Then, and only then, can you begin to write bullet statements about your accomplishments that will hit your target audience—your boss, a prospective employer, or a new contact you made. Your bullet statements should be used continually, as well as be placed in your *"I love me"* file, which you will use whenever you want to write a winning resume or prepare for an interview or a performance evaluation. You'll also have to price yourself according to what the market will bear and what you've discovered that you have to offer. Doing all of these things will enable you to set the self-marketing process in motion.

Chapter 4 Key Points

- Throw away the notion that there is only one right place and one right time for you to self market

- Realize that you're always in the right place at the right time; you just need to take advantage of the opportunities all around you

- Synergy involves focusing all of your energy on what you want and verbalizing your desires; when applied to your career, results are guaranteed

- Listing the places and times when you come in contact with people, both personally and professionally, will help you realize opportunities for self marketing abound

Techniques and Strategies for Being in the Right Place at the Right Time

4

You're most likely aware of the saying, *"You need to be in the right place at the right time."* We've heard many clients moan over the fact that they were in the wrong place, or that their timing was off even though the place was right. We don't buy that. The fact is that you're always in the right place at the right time. You're just not taking advantage of it.

How are you not taking advantage of it? Well, you might not be opening your mouth and talking, you might not be seeing the available opportunities, or you may be putting your energy into the wrong activities. Once you know how to take advantage of the opportunities around you, you'll see how obvious they are. It's kind of like buying a new car in a spectacular color and then seeing cars exactly like yours everywhere you go. You just never noticed them out there before you became aware that they existed.

Taking Advantage of Your Current Activities and Contacts

Many people are unaware of the opportunities around them. They're so focused on their current jobs and problems that they can't see beyond the blinders they have on. So much of *"being in the right place at the right time"* is understanding that every place is the right place, and every time is the right time for self marketing. There's not just one time and one place in your lifetime that is your ticket to career success. If that were the case, career success would be as improbable as winning the lottery jackpot.

Every day, in every way, you're in the right place at the right time. Most people get jobs through our program by learning how to self market successfully and then doing it every day and in all sorts of places. It's a concept worth learning. Most of our clients think we are going to teach them how to get a different or better job by answering a want ad. Not on your life. Not that it doesn't ever happen that way, but we've learned that if we can get you to become a walking-talking career-changer, magic happens.

You've probably relied on this concept many times in your personal life. One of our clients, Karen Goldman, told us how she was so interested in adopting a child, she told everyone she knew about her search. She ended up talking to acquaintances in parking lots, strangers at the tennis court, and friends of friends of friends over the telephone. *"Everyone started telling me stories of how they or people they knew adopted children,"* Karen said. *"And I got so much information and so many offers to adopt, I was literally overwhelmed."*

Think of the adage that anything or anybody you want to meet is only three phone calls away. The point is that you must start opening your mouth before things start happening. We tried the *"three phone call"* trial to see if we could meet a former president of

> *"If you fail, it's because you took a chance; if you succeed, it's because you grasped an opportunity."*
> Anonymous

the United States. We remembered that our sister's mother-in-law, who lived in Palm Desert, had a neighbor who was former President Gerry Ford's chief of staff. With three phone calls, we could most likely reach our goal. Who or what are you three phone calls away from?

What you need to do is make a concerted effort to be in the right place at the right time. Concentrating all of your efforts on achieving your goals is often described as synergy. When you are aware of what you want and make every effort to get it, you are behaving synergistically. The total effect of your combined energies is incredibly powerful.

> *A participant in one of our workshops, Michelle Chapman, told us about an experience she had after taking a course on synergy. "We learned that the more energy you put into the universe, the more comes back to you," she said. Michelle has four children, an eight-year-old, a ten-year-old, and two babies. "I also have a mountain of laundry. It just never ends," she shared. "I finally figured out that I could keep up with the washing end of it if only I had two dryers." The day after she took the course, Michelle said to her husband, who was going on a grocery run, "I could get to the end of this laundry pile if we just had another dryer." Michelle's husband came back with a near-new dryer in ten minutes. "There was a garage sale down the street," he said, "and they were selling this dryer for twenty dollars. I grabbed it." Michelle was initially astounded, but then realized, "I just had to verbalize what I needed. Had I not, my husband would have passed by that garage sale without a glance, and I'd still be stuck with my laundry pile."*

Can synergy work for you in your career? Absolutely. The more aware you are of what you need and want, and the more you verbalize those desires to others *(self marketing)*, the more in tune you and others will be with the opportunities around you. Self marketing enables you to get others on your team in order to get what you want. Synergy multiplies with self marketing.

Sam Calabrese, a participant in one of our workshops, tried the synergy concept for himself. He had decided that he would like to be a travel writer after retirement. *"I started to read travel magazines and noted the bylines,"* Sam said. *"Then, to everyone I came in contact with, I casually mentioned during conversation that I really liked to travel and asked if they knew anyone who made a living traveling. Within two weeks, I ended up meeting three travel writers."*

Have you ever had a similar experience? Perhaps you uncovered information or found something or someone you were looking for, simply because you were focused on the task and asked until you got the result you wanted. Write about that experience here.

_____

_____

_____

_____

_____

_____

_____

_____

_____

_____

> "Goals—write them down, hang them up, share them often—and watch them happen!"
> Anonymous

Techniques and Strategies for Being in the Right Place at the Right Time

If you have yet to experience what happens when you verbalize what you want or you would like more practice, try the following exercise. Pretend that you are going on a trip to Hawaii. Ask everyone you come in contact with if they have been to Hawaii. If so, ask if they can recommend places to visit. Write here about the results of your *"marketing survey."*

In the next chapter, we'll help you formulate the words you'll use to tell the world what you want. But you have to be willing to verbalize your desires, and you have to recognize that every day you come across people who can help you in your career. If you don't tell people what you want, they can't help you. The world goes by with you feeling left out, but it's not a matter of being in the wrong place or having it be the wrong time. You're simply not articulating what you want. You need to prioritize your self-marketing strategy.

Where Do You Hang Out?

It's our premise that you must self market everywhere in order to get the word out about who you are, what you can do, and what you want. To get comfortable with this tactic, we have our clients make a list of all the places they frequent. Then, when they find themselves in those particular environments, it registers that they should start to self market.

Where do you hang out? Usually the places you find yourself in can be divided into two categories—your personal life and your professional life.

Personal Life

In the pursuit of personal activities, where do you go? To the neighborhood market or the closest strip mall? Look at the list that we have started for you, and add the places you visit on the lines that follow. They may prove to be valuable places for meeting new contacts who could help you further your career.

I Can Contact People At...

Kids' soccer games

Church activities

Homeowner meetings

Orthodontist's waiting room

Gym

"We miss 100 percent of the orders we don't ask for."
Zig Ziglar

Marketing Yourself and Your Career

> *One of our clients, Leslie Boyle, took our workshop on self marketing to heart. At a Christmas play, she had to sit by herself because of limited seating and decided to test her self-marketing skills on the gentleman next to her, also separated from his party. "I started with a little chitchat about the play," Leslie said. "Soon he asked what I did for a living." Leslie told him she was a nurse who was looking for a career change, and she recited the marketing script we had helped her prepare. The man was a decision maker at a biomedical firm, and he arranged for her to interview for a position in customer service at his organization. Leslie took it. "If I hadn't prepared to self market myself in all kinds of situations, I would have closed myself off to an amazing opportunity," she told us.*

It's critical that you remember that you do need a marketing script. Without it, it doesn't matter where and when you decide to self market. Hang on. We will coach you through the process of developing your own self-marketing script in chapter five, so that you know exactly what to say to the people you run into. But for now, it's essential that you identify the places and times you can self market.

Professional Life

Now you'll make a list of where you could make contacts within your current organization. Think beyond the scope of your boss's office, and look for all the opportunities where you could self market.

I Can Self Market...

In the cafeteria

At a task-force meeting

In a volunteer committee

At a training class

In the elevator

Marketing Yourself and Your Career

> *Rick Endicott, a client of ours, was a teacher who did some teleconferencing for his school district. At a school fund-raiser, Rick decided to use his self-marketing skills. "Instead of telling people I was a teacher," he said, "I focused on the teleconferencing project I had just completed." One of his new contacts was a vice president at a large aerospace firm. "His firm was considering investing money in a teleconferencing center," Rick shared with us. "I gave him my business card, and he contacted me the following week. I met with the personnel director at his firm and was offered a job. I'm a living example of the power of self marketing."*

You're not going to get a job offer every time you open your mouth. However, if you verbalize your desire enough times, the odds are that someone who can do something for you, or who knows somebody who can, will listen and help you.

"My eventual goal is to build a spaceship and colonize Venus, but for now I'm looking to move into a senior consultant position."

Summary

You are in the right place, and the time is right. You just have to grasp the opportunities in front of you. If you learn to focus your energies on marketing yourself successfully in all situations, you'll experience the magic of synergy. We've seen it happen time and time again to a number of our clients, and there's nothing quite like it. Don't get left out. Take advantage of the very same good fortune with a successful self-marketing mix that includes *"place."*

Chapter 5 Key Points

- 🗝 Most people tend to say too little about themselves; learning how to capitalize on the power of words will boost your career

- 🗝 Self-marketing scripts give you the power to effectively articulate your career desires

- 🗝 It's your choice whether or not to play the *"dressing game"*; those who do play have a chance at winning

Presenting Yourself in a Positive Manner

5

Self marketing is a breeze if you have skills and accomplishments to talk about, and you know how to look and sound good in the process. You've already analyzed your skills and accomplishments in order to determine which ones to feature, you've set your price to match, and you realize that you have to self market continually and everywhere you go. You've done a great deal *(but not all)* of the necessary work. Hang in there. We'll see you through the rest of the self-marketing process.

To use marketing terminology, in this chapter we're going to have you work a bit more on your product package and your promotional efforts. First, we're going to teach you how to create a self-marketing script that works for you. Then we're going to ask you to critique your image, and encourage you, if necessary, to upgrade it.

Using the Power of Words to Gain a New Image and Visibility

You may be ready for a change—a new career, a promotion, or perhaps a different job within your organization. But have you made the necessary changes in how you talk about yourself? What you say about yourself—in introducing or talking about yourself—is so very critical to the self-marketing process. Many people have no idea of the power of the words that come out of their mouths. They're not even conscious of the fact that what they're saying or not saying is being judged.

So, take heed. What you say about yourself does impact your career. And even if you say nothing, that too is a statement that has great impact. In fact, more people say too little than too much. They're afraid of being labeled as braggarts or show-offs. Yet, only about 2 percent of the working population talks too much; the other 98 percent tries to do the opposite.

A participant in one of our workshops found it difficult to conceive of promoting herself verbally. *"My boss can see that I stay late, and I know she notices when I work especially hard on a project. Why isn't that enough?"* Good question. But while words without actions to back them up won't make an outstanding impression, actions without words often get overlooked. Don't leave your career to chance. You need to learn to use the power of words to make yourself visible and steer your career in the right direction.

We're going to give you some right and wrong ways to introduce yourself to others; then we'll teach you how to create your own self-marketing script.

> "Your voice is your second signature."
> R. I. Fitzhenry

Why should you use a self-marketing script?

Marketing yourself starts long before the job interview. When you are out talking to people about your various job options, you want to sound credible, believable, and directed. You also want to sound somewhat knowledgeable about the career field you're going after, so they will have confidence in you and give you leads and information.

If you don't sound very confident and if you don't sound like you know where you are going, people aren't going to be eager or willing to help you. Your major task and challenge is to help others see your personal connection with what you want to do and the skills, experiences, and knowledge that you have. That is why we have the self-marketing script—to make it easier for you to do this. The self-marketing script forces you to look over all your career options and critically think about and analyze all the ways in which your skills and your past experiences relate to this career option.

If you've ever attended a professional meeting, you've noticed that time is allotted for people to introduce themselves. It does have to be done rather quickly, because time is of the essence, but most or all of the people never say anything remarkable or significant. If you have a self-marketing script, you can take advantage of this self-marketing opportunity. Don't let yourself slip by unnoticed.

Usually, about 10 percent of the people that attend a professional meeting are in career transition. They don't have a job. Self introductions take on maximum importance if you're out of work. Yet, many of these people fall back on boring introductions: *"Hi, my name is Rex Stanford. I'm in transition. I'm an HR generalist, and I'm looking for a job here in this county."*

"Can't figure out how to get where you're going? Remember how you got where you are now."
Anonymous

> "Have the daring to see yourself as a bundle of possibilities."
> Harry Emerson Fosdick

Those who listen to Rex's introduction don't know what to do with it. Maybe there are ninety people in the group. They may know of an opening, but by the time the other nine people who are out of work say the same thing, they've forgotten all about Rex. And, actually, none of the nine stand out.

Now try this introduction on for size. *"Hi, I'm Rex Stanford. I've spent fifteen years in Human Resources in a wide variety of industries. My special expertise is creating human-resource systems that work for both the employees and the organization. I would welcome an opportunity to talk to any of you who have an opening that would take advantage of my skills."*

Isn't that introduction far more meaningful and much more powerful? We'll show you how to create your own self-marketing script in a minute or two; just stick with us while we reveal the difference between a ho-hum introduction that gets lost in the shuffle and a targeted one that gets results.

Rex made himself stand out from the others by using words that applied to him and his situation. He didn't choose trite, over-used phrases. And he didn't seem boastful, nor did he threaten anyone.

> *We attend many professional meetings, and we see introductions done in all different ways. The vast majority are done incorrectly. In fact, we were at an ASTD (American Society for Training and Development) meeting when we heard an introduction we tell clients never to use. Many public school teachers attend ASTD meetings to see if they'd like to transition to training in corporations. Everyone at our table had to introduce themselves, and a number of the people in our group were teachers. One woman introduced herself by name, then said, "I am just a high school band teacher." Her statement was self-deprecating and unenlightening. Not one person at that table would even think about hiring her. She could have said: "Hi, my name is Mary Smith.*

> *I have been an educator and trainer for twelve years. My most recent experience has been with adolescents. I would welcome an opportunity to use my training skills with adults. I look forward to joining this group and volunteering my meeting-and-events planning skills for the many events that ASTD sponsors."* Had she said that, some people at the table would be thinking, "I could see her making a transition to my field." Others would think, "I have a committee for her to join." And still others might be thinking, "I'd like to help her, because she's willing to help us."

One of the best networking opportunities for people in corporations is to take classes. But what amazes us is that most people go to their classes, sit in the back, and never say a word to anyone. They miss out on a great opportunity to self market. Sure, they *(hopefully)* pick up a body of knowledge that will help them in their careers, but they don't take advantage of a tremendous self-marketing situation.

In a class, the first impression you make is usually in your self introduction. It's a rare corporate class where people don't introduce themselves. Most people in a class say something like, *"Hi. I'm Joe Gonzalez, and I'm from engineering."* Then the other twenty-nine people in the class follow Joe's example and say something very similar. It's a fact of human nature. We follow the pattern set for us, whether the instructor presents a model for introducing oneself or the first person to introduce does.

Do you want to stand out in a positive manner? Then do something different. Wouldn't it be much more effective if Joe said, *"Good morning. I'm Joe Gonzalez. I currently work in the engineering department. I was part of a team that recently completed a project I'm sure many of you heard about—our downtown redevelopment that just won a*

"You don't get a second chance to make a first impression."
Anonymous

national award." Joe is more than an engineer to us now. He's not taking full credit for the successful redevelopment project, but he has let us know that he's connected to a project that we're already aware of. We will remember him.

You may not want anything from the people in your class at this moment. But when an opportunity or an opening comes up, you want those people to remember you. You want to stand out from the crowd in a positive way.

Career transitions are described in great detail in our book, *Making Career Transitions*. But we do want to show you now how your words can help you make that change before it actually takes place. One of our clients, Jim Brown, worked for a small engineering firm. He decided, through the assessment process, that he wanted to be in the financial planning industry. He located and attended a meeting of financial planners—the International Association of Financial Planners.

Jim told us, *"If you hadn't told me about my marketing mix and instructed me on how to create a marketing script, I would have walked into that meeting, recited my name, and told those attending that I was an engineer. Instead, I said, 'Hi, I'm Jim Brown. I'm currently an engineer for a major oil company. I'm exploring a career change into financial planning. I'm excited about this opportunity, because I've been investing in the stock market and planning my own finances since I was sixteen years old.'"*

Do you get it? Jim captured the attention of all those at the meeting. With his choice of words, he was able to place himself above other job seekers who hadn't planned what they were going to say.

> "If you don't let others know what you want, it will remain a secret."
> Victoria Nauss

When and where do you use a self-marketing script?

Your self-marketing script can be used both on and off the job. When you are on the job, you may opt to use your script:

- at meetings
- at volunteer opportunities inside your company
- during training courses
- when meeting someone new in the cafeteria
- on a company sports team

Outside of your company, you can use your self-marketing script:

- at professional meetings
- on job interviews
- at social occasions
- at community volunteer activities

Trust your good sense and judgment. If you feel you're not in an appropriate time or place to introduce yourself in this way, don't. Read people, watch your environment, and check your intuition. For example, some people who sit next to you on an airplane don't want to be bothered. If someone has his laptop in front of his face and doesn't ever look in your direction, don't thrust yourself on him.

One of our clients, Troy Wentworth, who worked in the real estate department of a major corporation, chose to serve on a committee within his department that was looking at its own reorganization within the corporation. Troy had a very caring attitude toward the people who were going to be affected by the reorganization. A vice president was sitting in on the first committee meeting where Troy introduced himself by saying: "Hi. I'm Troy Wentworth, and I've been with the real estate department for the last five years. I was asked to participate in the reorganization activities of the department; and I, along with a small group, designed a system that met the needs of both the displaced employees and the organization. My input was to ensure that the displaced employees got the very best possible care." The vice president took note of Troy, who then ended up on a managerial task force that planned the major reorganization of the corporation for three months before it was actually rolled out. During this time, Troy reported directly to the chairman of the board.

Creating Self-Marketing Scripts

Your self-marketing script, carefully prepared, will put you ahead of the game when introducing yourself in a networking group, responding to questions in a job interview, or when describing your skills to someone in a social situation. Your script will tell others that you are qualified and appropriate for your chosen career or position. It will show the match between what's required for the job you're after and your skills, experiences, and qualities.

It's much easier to market yourself and say your lines if you've thought of the lines beforehand and have practiced them. That's why we want you to understand what goes into a self-marketing script and why we want you to create your own and practice it.

Presenting Yourself in a Positive Manner

Your self-marketing script will tell others:

1. where you are now, your past experiences, and what has made you special and successful in your current role
2. where you are going—your general or specific career goal
3. the skills and qualities you have to take with you.

When we interview successful clients and ask them what was one of their most helpful self-marketing practices, they often state that it was the opportunity to start talking about themselves and presenting themselves before they were actually on the job interview. Their self-marketing scripts gave them the confidence to begin this. A job interview can be tension-producing, but if you've had practice presenting yourself and know your lines, it becomes less stressful and, perhaps, even fun.

Before you can do a good job of writing your marketing script and presenting yourself, you must think through your past skills, experiences, and knowledge to see which are related to your targeted career option.

Pretend that you're an employer and need to fill a position such as the one you're looking at. List any transferable skills, any technical skills, and any knowledge or experience that would be helpful or required for the job. Take sales, for example. You'd need to know about marketing; the product you're selling; a knowledge of sales techniques *(what it means to qualify the buyer or overcome objections and close for the sale)*; good communication, persuasive, and interpersonal skills; the ability to train and educate people; and effective time-management skills. As far as characteristics and qualities are concerned, you'd need to be a self starter, motivated by money, enthusiastic, willing to withstand rejection, and a quick learner.

See how your own skills and experiences link. If you've read *Unlocking Your Career Potential*, you can refer to your accomplishment stories, your transferable-skills list, and your career checklist.

Your background statement

Your background statement is a brief summary of either your prior experience or your current job. It's just a way of letting people know where you've been or where you are. Use whatever is appropriate. If your current job is most reflective of your skills for the position you're after, use that. In some instances, it will be stronger to summarize other work experiences.

For example, a teacher who wanted to work in sales wrote in her self-marketing script: *"I have a background in retail sales, commission-only sales, and currently I'm an educator where I sell to students, staff, and administrators every day."* A county worker chose the following tactic: *"Currently I work for the county in the human services department. My major responsibilities include the development and implementation of training programs for the staff. I enjoy this aspect of my work and therefore am considering training and development as a career transition."*

Do yourself justice and don't undersell what you can do. In some cases, a title doesn't work very well. Either it's very general or it truly doesn't reflect the breadth and scope of your position. In such cases, it's perfectly acceptable to describe the functions of the work you perform instead of your actual title.

> *A young woman who was an employee of a bookstore had a title of "clerk," but was actually in charge of one of the departments of the bookstore, which was a large chain that sold religious books. It was a very successful company. Instead of saying that she was a store clerk, she said: "I work for a large, specialized, nationally-known bookstore chain. I am responsible for managing one department, and I also do all the purchasing of supplies. I interact with the public a good deal of the time." Instead of being tied to a menial title, she revealed her management function and the breadth of her position.*

Another client was a media specialist for a school. Some people might think such a job merely involved threading a film projector. However, this woman had become involved in computers and had broad responsibilities for selecting and purchasing computers for the district. So, we had her say: *"Currently I'm a media specialist for XYZ school. My major responsibility is the selection and purchasing of computers for all our business and learning systems."* She described her responsibilities to adequately reflect the scope of her job duties.

Where you're headed

In your self-marketing script, you also need to identify where you are going. Are you looking to expand what you currently do, find a similar position in a different industry, or totally change careers? Your listener can't help you unless you verbalize what you want.

If you can be more specific about what you really want to do, the person that you're talking to can do a better job of helping you. For example, if you're going into sales and know that you'd like to sell a service, or product that's part of a service, and you know you want more than one contact with a customer, you could say something like: *"I prefer to sell a service, or a product that's part of a*

"When you know where you're going, tell others. They might have directions for getting there."
Debbie Cahoon

service. I want a sales position that allows me to have an ongoing relationship with my customers; and, although I'm open, I'm currently interested in food and recreation industries." It's not always possible to be this specific, but do it if you can, because it certainly will make your search more successful.

A person who is going into training and development might already have discovered that he or she doesn't want to do just stand-up training, so he or she might say something like: *"I would like to perform the program development and implementation function as well as stand-up training."*

Summary of your skills

What you'd like to leave your listener with is a summary of your skills. The person or the people you're talking to may be able to infer your skills by the other things you have said, but you never want to count on inferences to make your point. We counsel our clients to be very clear and even repetitive if they need to be.

For example, the teacher who wanted a position in sales might say, *"In summary, I feel I bring communication, interpersonal, educational, and training skills to the field of sales. In addition, I'm motivated, I'm a self starter, and I'm quick to learn."*

For a person who would like to pursue a position in public affairs: *"I bring to the field of issues management and public affairs the ability to research, write, identify critical issues, and communicate them effectively. Interpersonal and communication skills are part of my repertoire, and I have the ability to deal with a variety of people from business executives to the community at large. I also have management and organizational skills."*

Samples of self-marketing scripts

In some situations you'll use a longer version of your self-marketing script; in others, a short one is what makes sense. That's why we've included samples of each. Read through the samples until you get a good feel for what's involved in a self-marketing script.

Longer script for interviews:

"I'm Bob Jones. My background includes conceptualizing and managing a preschool, and initiating and coordinating adolescent programs in psychiatric hospitals. The success of these programs was due in great part to my marketing and public relations activities. I'm in a career transition, focusing on public relations and/or community relations in the health field for an educational institution."

Shorter version for introductions at meetings:

"I'm Bob Jones. My background includes managing and promoting a preschool and adolescent programs in psychiatric hospitals. I'm in a career transition, focusing on public relations and/or community relations in the health field for an educational institution."

Longer script for interviews:

"I'm Morgan Stratford. I have worked in sales on a commission-only basis for seven-and-a-half years. My work has included the coordination and staging of public relations events. I'm enthusiastic and highly motivated about a career in sales. I am a good representative of any organization, and I can easily establish rapport with people and define the needs of my customers. I'm seeking a new challenge in sales and am interested in both product and service sales with a possible emphasis on promotion."

Shorter version for introductions at meetings:

"I'm Morgan Stratford. I have worked in sales on a commission-only basis for seven-and-a-half years. This work has included the coordination and staging of public relations events. I'm exploring different kinds of sales and promotions and would be interested in talking to those who are in the field of sales."

Longer script for interviews:

"I'm Robert Mullen, and I work for a large, specialized bookstore, well recognized in its industry. I function as a department manager, resource and reference person, coordinator of inventory supplies and purchasing, and I'm also in sales and promotion. I'm looking for a position in the community-service field that would use my leadership, public relations, organizational, and marketing skills. My past involvement in community-service projects has shown my interest and skill in this area, and my expertise as a manager, resourcer, and promoter are a natural transfer to community service."

Shorter version for introductions at meetings:

"I'm Robert Mullen, and I function as a department manager for a national bookstore. Plus, I have much experience in community service. I'm looking for a position in the community-service field that would use my leadership, public relations, organizational, and marketing skills."

Now you'll get to practice writing a marketing script for someone else.

Can You Compose a Marketing Script?

One of our clients, an administrative assistant, was interested in pursuing a career in property management. Look at the following duties that she had to carry out in her position as an administrative assistant. Then check those experiences which most directly apply to her desired career in property management.

_____ Recruited and hired clerical staff

_____ Set staff schedules

_____ Organized board meetings

_____ Was responsible for accounting, insurance, budget

_____ Reviewed contracts

_____ Maintained computer data bases

_____ Managed the general office and various projects

_____ Interfaced with clients, vendors, business associates, the banker, and accountant

_____ Helped computerize the office

_____ Oversaw the expansion and decorating of the office

_____ Dealt with the city planning department

_____ Negotiated with painters and the carpet company

_____ Revised the performance-review system

Now write a short marketing script for this person.

_____

_____

_____

Marketing Yourself and Your Career

> How did that go? Are you ready to try your own self-marketing script? Select a career area you're interested in. What skills and experiences does this career require? List them.
>
> ✏️ _____
> _____
> _____
> _____
> _____
> _____
>
> Which of your skills and experiences most directly apply to this career?
>
> ✏️ _____
> _____
> _____
> _____
> _____
> _____

Create a self-marketing script you could use to let others know that you're interested in this new career area; it should reveal the skills and abilities that make you a good candidate for the new position. Use words that are comfortable for you.

Presenting Yourself in a Positive Manner

My Self-Marketing Script

Longer Version

_____
_____
_____
_____
_____
_____
_____
_____
_____
_____
_____

Short Version

_____
_____
_____
_____
_____

Using your self-marketing script becomes more natural and easier to recite with time. You'll become used to knowing how much to recite depending on the situation. In a social situation, you'll probably start with a quick summary, such as, *"I'm in career transition, and I'm looking at sales."* Your partner may ask a question you can respond to, such as, *"Oh, what's your background?"* or *"Well, why are you interested in sales?"* You'll be able to respond to any question, because you've prepared your self-marketing script in advance.

If you're at an association meeting, and you have to introduce yourself, you most likely will give the short version that states your background and ends with, *"I'd like to talk to anyone in the field of sales."* If you're in an information interview, you can usually recite the longer version of your self-marketing script. It all depends on the situation.

Take the time to create a self-marketing script that feels comfortable and that works for you. Next, practice, practice some more, and keep practicing until it becomes second nature. Then unleash the power of your words on as many people as you can.

Upgrading Your Personal Presentation

> "It's not just what we say, but how we look while we're saying it, that makes others interested in our message."
> Vikki Sparks

The image that you project greatly influences those around you. When you are confident about how you look and the image you portray, your personal effectiveness increases. Your personality and your self image are magnified by the way you look.

We run across many people who are resentful of or unhappy about the fact that their personal image makes such a difference. But it does. If *"dressing for success"* makes you uncomfortable, please realize that in some environments you won't go very far unless you do dress for success.

However, if you really do not enjoy dressing professionally, you should look for companies that have a casual dress environment. They do exist. We know of one company where everyone, the CEO included, wears jeans. So if this is a point of contention with you, search out an environment where you fit in.

In most organizations, the higher you go, the dressier it gets. But it's up to you whether or not you want to join the *"dressing game."* If you don't want to move up the ladder in an organization that does play the dressing game, you don't have to. It's your choice.

The only exception to this rule is if you are high enough on the totem pole in your organization *(perhaps the owner)*, or if you bring something to an organization that no one else does. In such cases, you can ignore the rules of the dressing game. We've seen some scientists who actually dress like mad scientists. But they know they can't be replaced. The majority of people still have to play by the rules.

Some of our clients go on and on about how phony the whole game is. Since we dress professionally when we conduct our workshops, if our clients protest too much about projecting a professional image, we stop them and say: *"Okay, you've formulated an impression about us in the time we've spent with you. We enjoy talking with you, and we can tell that you like the class. But what if we came into this room dressed in shorts? What would you have thought?"* This scenario stops most of them in their tracks. The fact is that they would be very disconcerted if we led our workshops dressed in shorts.

Marketing Yourself and Your Career

At a major corporation that was downsizing, a number of employees were told that they had three months to find a new position within the organization, or they would be outplaced. Most of these employees had worked in regional offices where the dress was informal, and they were brought to headquarters where the dress was much more formal. One employee recounted the difference in dress: "I was used to wearing jeans and cowboy boots at my office, and suddenly I was thrust into an environment of suits and ties. It was a shock to my system." Twenty-five of the thirty employees made the transition to formal dress and got jobs within the organization. The five who continued to dress exactly as they had prior to the downsizing lost their jobs.

We would like you to answer the following questions so that you can think about how you feel about your image and dress, and what you might do about it. This isn't a dress-for-success course. It's just that we cannot talk about presenting yourself in a positive manner without addressing the issue of image. It's not possible.

My Personal Presentation

How much do you know about the importance of personal and professional images? Think about the following questions; then answer them according to how you see yourself and how you perceive others see you.

1. What image does the career or job you have targeted require?

   _____

   _____

   _____

Presenting Yourself in a Positive Manner

2. Does your personal image, at this time, fit the image of the career you are seeking?

_____
_____

3. If not, what actions need to be taken to assist you to change into the new career image?

_____
_____
_____
_____
_____

4. Do you ask yourself whom you are going to meet and what you are going to do before you get dressed?

_____
_____

5. Do you believe that everything you wear sends a message—whether positive or negative?

_____
_____

Marketing Yourself and Your Career

6. What are your impressions of someone you meet for the first time?

_____

_____

_____

_____

7. By what standards do you form your opinions?

_____

_____

_____

_____

8. To what degree does a person's visual image affect you when your first meet him or her?

_____

_____

_____

_____

Presenting Yourself in a Positive Manner

9. State three adjectives people use when they meet you:

   a. _____

   b. _____

   c. _____

10. To what degree do different situations require differences in image with the style of clothes, colors, and accessories? For example, what would one wear to a job interview versus an evening social event?

   _____

   _____

   _____

   _____

11. Do you dress for the job you have or the job you want?

   _____

   _____

12. Do you know how to dress *(what to wear)* to get that new job or promotion?

   _____

   _____

Part of knowing what to wear for success in your chosen position or career involves research. If you're after a promotion, how does the person in the position you're after dress? If you're considering a career change, check out how the people dress in the industry or company in which you're interested. When image is at stake, just being observant can provide you with more than enough information. Or you can ask someone you respect for suggestions. Dressing as you should for the career or position you want will boost your promotional efforts.

One of our clients, Nick Harris, was getting an MBA while working as a sales manager for a construction company. At his construction job, he wore jeans. Because Nick had such a great interest in the stock market, he became an intern for his economics professor. *"I thought it would be a way to break into the financial field,"* Nick said. He was doing everything possible to make the transition to the financial field, except for his dress. *"Since I went straight from my construction job to the university, I was always dressed in jeans,"* he shared. We convinced Nick to dress like his professor and his classmates, who came to school in their professional clothes. *"You'll get a much better response,"* we said. And he did. *"My classmates afforded me more respect,"* Nick told us, *"and, some months later, my professor offered me a job."*

"Work experiences are often portable. You can take them from one career to another."
Anonymous

Presenting Yourself in a Positive Manner

Summary

Looking good and saying the right things won't do everything for you, but they just may give you the push you need to get the promotion you want or the position you've been after. Don't disregard the power of the words that come out of your mouth or the power of the image you project. Create a self-marketing script that promotes you well and that is comfortable to recite. Then practice it and perform it. And remember to upgrade your product package. It's all part of the marketing mix that you are creating to increase your ability to choose the career or position you want.

"I'd like to be yuppied up."

Chapter 6 Key Points

🗝 Promoting yourself within your organization means more than upward mobility; it also refers to lateral moves, moves down the ladder to take advantage of a different opportunity, and enriching your present job

🗝 Some people distrust job-posting systems, but they provide an excellent opportunity to promote yourself and to make a desired move

🗝 Not everyone is ready to climb the corporate ladder

🗝 If you schedule a career conversation with your manager on a yearly basis, you can help your career along

🗝 Try to enrich your career on your terms before it gets enlarged for you by someone else

🗝 Take advantage of the numerous marketing strategies available to you

Promoting Yourself within Your Own Organization

6

It could be that you're not interested in changing careers. Maybe you don't even want to switch industries or organizations. You really like the company you work for; your only gripe is that you don't want to stay in the same position doing the same things for the rest of your life. We hear such statements from our clients on a regular basis. Some already feel stuck; others just want information for when they're ready to make a move in their organizations.

When we tell our clients that we're going to help them promote themselves within their own organizations, they immediately think we're talking about moving up the career ladder to a higher position. Certainly, many of our clients are interested in such a move, but that's a limited view of the whole promotion issue. We also see promotion as promoting yourself in the same position you're in now, promoting yourself laterally, or even promoting yourself to a new opportunity by moving down the ladder to regroup and see where you want to go next.

> "The method of the enterprising is to plan with audacity, and execute with vigor; to sketch out a map of possibilities; and then to treat them as probabilities."
> — Bovee

In this chapter, we'll first explore lateral moves and discuss why you should use some of the more formal systems like job posting to find opportunities. Then we'll look at the realities of climbing up the ladder, check out the possible benefits of climbing down, and reveal the many ways you can grow in place before you make another move. Whichever way you decide to turn in your organization, it's vital that you have an annual career conversation with your boss or manager. It will keep the two of you up-to-date on where you're headed. And finally, we want to leave you with an action-oriented marketing list. It will encourage you to get started on self marketing.

Making a Lateral Move

A lateral move is a good option to consider, because it can result in a win-win situation for both the employee and the organization. If you choose to make a lateral move, you get a new career, new challenges, new skills, new people to interact with, and you do not risk leaving your organization, which is a *"known"* to you. Your company also benefits. It gets a rejuvenated employee who is already socialized within the organizational culture.

Many of our clients have wisely chosen lateral moves. One young woman discovered through the career-assessment process that she wasn't cut out for her current position in customer service. *"I couldn't stand the constant contact with irate customers,"* she explained. *"So I bided my time until an opening came up in purchasing. It was a much better match for my skills. I applied, got it, and am happy I didn't leave the company."* Her story is one of many we hear from clients who made lateral moves and knew it was the right choice for them.

Smart companies, if they are large enough, promote lateral moves through a job-posting system. Opportunities are formally posted, enabling all employees to see what the opportunities are and to apply for them, if they desire. If there is a job-posting system in your organization and you're interested in making a lateral move, use it.

Job-posting systems are designed to make the internal job-hunting process more objective and systematic. In a small company without a job-posting system, employees have to rely on informal word-of-mouth to hear about any upcoming job opportunities. A job-posting system provides equal opportunity for all those interested in a different job. Of course, no system is totally objective nor totally fair.

Participants in our workshops sometimes complain about the job-posting systems in their organizations. *"It's not fair,"* we hear them say. Well, job-posting systems are as fair as any system a human being creates. People think they are unfair because only one person out of all those who apply for the job gets it. Only one person per posted position ends up happy. If ten people apply for a job in human resources, one person hears *"yes"* and nine people hear *"no."*

Now, if those nine really thought through what they got out of the experience, they would agree that the system does work. It allows the organization to look at ten candidates, and it gives ten people the opportunity to put their best foot forward. Unfortunately, an organization can only choose one candidate. In the absence of a formal system, rejection is easier because you don't necessarily know if you have been considered. It's less fair and less objective, but you don't experience an outright rejection because you never formally apply for the job. However, no matter how fair or unfair you think the job-posting system in your organization is, it's probably well worth using.

"The world belongs to the optimists; pessimists are only spectators."
Francois Guizot

> "He who desires to learn has to first overcome the fear of failure."
> — Anonymous

The biggest objection to a job-posting system is the perception that there is an inside candidate who is already slated for the job, but the organization wants to appear fair, so it interviews all who want to apply. It's absurd to think there are no inside candidates. Managers are paid to spot talent. But if a manager still attempts to be as objective as possible, the system will work. You just have to get over the notion that a job-posting system eliminates the idea of an inside candidate.

What you have to decide is whether or not you want to enter a contest you may not win. It's the same as when you apply for a job outside your organization. You may get it; you may not. But whatever the outcome, it's still a good learning experience, especially for those who want to improve their self-marketing skills.

Why should you take advantage of your company's job-posting system? We tell our clients that there are four good reasons why they should. Take note of them:

1. If you don't play, you can't win. If you don't apply, you won't get the job. You can't make any moves by sitting on the bench. Your odds improve the moment you step into the game.

2. It gives you incredible practice in getting your resume *(and bullet statements)* together and in honing your interviewing skills. It's also another opportunity to use your self-marketing script. The more you do such self-marketing activities, the better you get at them.

3. You get a chance to see what the job is like. You can look at another department, and test whether or not you'd like to work there.

4. You get tremendous exposure. Even if you're second or third in the running, you've been introduced to someone you don't know. You can perform for someone who may remember you when another opportunity comes up.

> *Jill Blandman, one of our clients, was interested in making a lateral move in her organization, a mail-order company. She was a shipping supervisor, but had decided that a career move to catalogue production would interest her more. "A job opening in that department was posted on our system," Jill told us, "and I heard that another employee was a strong contender for the position. So, at first, I was hesitant to apply, but then I remembered the reasons you gave for trying the system regardless of who was in the running. I did great in the interview, and came in second." As it turned out, the manager was so impressed with Jill, that when he had another opening, he didn't post the job but called and offered it directly to her.*

The Realities of Climbing the Ladder

What if you're interested in climbing up in your organization? The messages you've heard from your parents, from school, and from society at large on the subject of climbing the corporate ladder are strikingly similar: *"Success is measured by how fast you climb it, and how close you get to the top."* Oh, sure, some parents say their only concern is that you're happy, but they certainly aren't thrilled with a lousy report card or a pink slip from your employer, no matter how happy you appear to be.

Before we get into the details of promoting yourself upward within your organization, we suggest you decide whether it's really what you want or need. In reality, climbing the corporate ladder is becoming more difficult as organizations are getting flatter. You need to determine your own definition of success. If that includes moving up, fine. If not, that's fine also.

"I cannot give you the formula for success, but I can give you the formula for failure—which is: Try to please everybody."
Herbert Bayard Swope

Marketing Yourself and Your Career

If moving up is not in your immediate future, don't stop reading. Your attitude often changes as your life and your needs change. In our workshops, a few people raise their hands when we pose the question, *"Is anyone here not interested in promotion or moving up?"* Some new mothers aren't. But when their children get older, they're ready to get off the *"mommy track."* Most everyone will need the information in this chapter at some point in their lives.

Are you cut out for the climb? Some people look at the goal and don't even consider what it takes to get there. It certainly looks fun in the executive suite. They've got big offices, more money, more benefits, nice cars, etc. The list could go on and on. But what do the people at the top have to pay for such luxuries? Time and energy. Most organizations extract more time and energy from their top people.

Make sure that you know the trade-offs for moving up, and make a conscious decision about whether or not you want to pay the price. Many people make the move with relish. But before we encourage our clients to go after it with gusto, we ask that they examine the cost.

Take the following quiz to get an idea of whether or not you'd be willing to work your way up the ladder.

> *"Success means getting your 'but' out of the way."*
> Anonymous

Am I Cut Out for the Corporate Climb?

Check whether you agree or disagree with each of the following statements.

Agree____ Disagree ____ 1. My personal life takes a minimum amount of my time.

Agree____ Disagree ____ 2. I am willing to work more than a forty-hour week.

Agree____ Disagree ____ 3. I want to work outside my job description.

Agree____ Disagree ____ 4. I enjoy taking on new tasks and responsibilities.

Agree____ Disagree ____ 5. I don't mind serving on task forces and committees and attending meetings.

Agree____ Disagree ____ 6. I don't mind taking responsibility for other people's work.

Agree____ Disagree ____ 7. I'm ready to be held accountable for more end results.

Agree____ Disagree ____ 8. I tend to see and think in the big picture.

Agree____ Disagree ____ 9. I'm ready for more interaction with customers, clients, and/or upper management.

Agree____ Disagree ____ 10. I am comfortable in new situations and welcome change.

Agree____ Disagree ____ 11. I enjoy working without direct supervision.

Agree____ Disagree ____ 12. I can manage my own time and schedule.

Agree____ Disagree ____ 13. I understand that I may be viewed differently by my colleagues and peers.

Agree____ Disagree ____ 14. I constantly look for new educational and training opportunities, done on company time or my own personal time.

Agree____ Disagree ____ 15. I am eager to contribute to my field through professional organizations.

Marketing Yourself and Your Career

Scoring Key

Count the number of times you checked *"agree."*

11-15: You most likely are ready for promotion and/or are already attempting the climb. Read through this chapter to learn how to maneuver the heights more easily.

6-10: Think through your reasons for wanting to climb the corporate ladder. You may decide to implement our ideas more slowly, choose a lateral move, or prepare to climb sometime in the future.

0-5: You're not ready at this time. Don't attempt the hike until you're comfortable with the realities involved and can put up with the pitfalls.

Some of our clients opt to move down the career ladder. In old terminology, that used to be called a demotion. It's now referred to as realignment. Realignment is a more positive term, because it more specifically defines moves that align you with your desires, skills, and aptitude. It's often a very positive step if you choose it yourself, and you have a very good reason for choosing it.

A college professor we know chose to give up her position, along with its title, demands, and benefits, to become a college instructor. She opted for realignment because she didn't want to expend her energy and time on pursuing a doctorate. Other clients choose to move down the ladder because they prefer the work in a lower position, or because they want time to pursue hobbies or self-employment opportunities, time which usually isn't available in higher positions.

> *David Krosby, a participant in one of our workshops who worked for a major computer corporation, discovered through assessing his career that he was climbing the corporate ladder and didn't want to. Most companies "reward" employees by moving them up, giving them more work, a title, more responsibility for others' work, and higher pay. David told us, "I learned through your class that I thoroughly enjoyed technical work. I didn't enjoy supervising others who did the work I loved." David elected to go back to his original position (i.e., he chose realignment). And he's much happier.*

Are you interested in moving up, in making a lateral move, or are you considering realignment? Maybe you'd prefer staying in your current position, but you'd like to change a few of your tasks Stick with us as we prepare you to be successful wherever you want to be in your organization.

Working Smart and Getting Where You Want to Be

Many people mistakenly think that a promotion means a totally new job with brand-new responsibilities. That's usually not the way it works. If you've been promoted, it's much more likely that you've already been handling many of the responsibilities that are attached to your new position or job title. You generally ease into a new position.

"*This is good news,*" we tell our clients. Why? Because it means that you can often work your way into a promotion or a lateral move within your organization; or, you can gain skills to make a move outside your organization. But it requires that you work smart and take advantage of job enrichment.

> "Here is a simple but powerful rule...always give people more than they expect to get."
> Nelson Boswell

"Job enrichment?" you ask. *"Sounds like a fancy term. What is it?"* Well, it's actually a good description, because it refers to a conscious choice on your part to enrich your job. It means changing your present position to expand the scope, visibility, autonomy, challenge, attractiveness, meaningfulness, and/or learning potential of your job. We know that's a mouthful, but it's the only way to describe job enrichment that does it justice.

It's called job enrichment, because it differs from job enlargement in that **you** decide to change your job because **you** want to. You take the initiative to change your job, and you can change the quality as well as the quantity of tasks. Job enlargement is someone else's choice to increase the tasks you do. For example, let's say that you currently do tasks A, B, and C. Your boss comes to you and says, *"You're a busy person, but I think you can also handle tasks D, E, and F."* Congratulations! Your job has just been enlarged.

Job enlargement happens to everybody all the time. Job enrichment is different. Job enrichment allows you to transform your job into one that's more enjoyable, more challenging, or more meaningful to you.

In job enrichment, you're currently handling tasks A, B, and C, and you go to your boss and say, *"I've got tasks A, B, and C wired. I'd also like to do D and E."* You have initiated it, and you have chosen the tasks you want added to your job. In the best of all possible worlds, your boss says, *"Well, let's go ahead and give tasks A and B to someone else."* Sometimes you get to lose some tasks you don't care about, but you must be prepared to do it all.

Job enrichment can include one or a combination of the following strategies:

1. Improving your present performance by identifying an area of weakness and deliberately working on that weakness. *(Example: If you're not really strong on a particular computer program, you opt to take a software class on company time or your own time.)*

2. Taking on a task, a project, or an event that you find enjoyable and that builds on a particular strength or skill. *(Example: After taking the software class, you're a whiz on the computer program, so you offer to teach the rest of your department.)*

3. Taking on a task, a project, or an event that allows you to learn and try an *"untried"* skill. *(Example: Perhaps your company is offering a course on public speaking; you decide to take it, because you have no experience in public speaking.)*

4. Taking on a task, a project, or an event that will allow you greater recognition and credibility within your organization. *(Example: Since your organization's big push this year is to work with the Girl Scouts, you decide to join the committee that will be the liaison between your organization and the Girl Scouts.)*

5. Asking for an opportunity to take total responsibility for a task, a project, or an event that you now do only a part of.

"Behold the turtle. He makes progress only when he sticks his neck out."
James B. Conant

Marketing Yourself and Your Career

> *One of our clients, Lani Glenn, was a medical technical writer for a major pharmaceutical company. She decided to use strategy #4—taking on a task, project, or event that would allow her greater recognition and credibility. Lani volunteered to be part of a committee that put on her organization's major annual conference for doctors. "For three years, I worked on the committee," Lani said, "and I kept up my technical writing work at the same time." She took on more and more responsibility every year. "Finally, I was ready for strategy #5—taking on total responsibility for a task, project, or event," Lani told us. "I went to my boss and said, 'If there's an opening, I would like to have the job that takes full responsibility for the major conference.' And I got it. I left my technical writing behind and became the meeting planner for the conference."*

You've no doubt enriched your career before. You just didn't know what it was called. You've probably asked to take on a certain responsibility or elected to take a course that would help you learn new skills. What we want you to do is to be conscious of your job-enrichment efforts.

In the past, when and how have you enriched your job?

_____
_____
_____
_____
_____
_____

Promoting Yourself within Your Own Organization

Which job-enrichment strategy is the most viable for you right now? Check one.

_____ 1. Improving your present performance by identifying an area of weakness and deliberately working on that weakness.

_____ 2. Taking on a task, a project, or an event that you find enjoyable and that builds on a particular strength or skill.

_____ 3. Taking on a task, a project, or an event that allows you to learn and try an *"untried"* skill.

_____ 4. Taking on a task, a project, or an event that will allow you greater recognition and credibility within your organization.

_____ 5. Asking for an opportunity to take total responsibility for a task, a project, or an event that you now do only a part of.

Describe how you would use the strategy you chose.

_____
_____
_____
_____
_____
_____

"Good opportunities are often disguised as hard labor. That's why so few people recognize them."
Ann Landers

By now, you are well aware that if you enrich your job, it will take time on your part. But it also allows you to get ready for a promotion, get visibility for a promotion, make your job more interesting, and/or gain new skills that may help you procure a new job inside or outside of your organization. In most organizations, your job is going to be enlarged anyway. We encourage our clients to take the bull by the horns and enrich it first.

Consider an organization that is being reorganized, and everyone has to start fresh in their new departments. In such a situation, our clients have the advantage, because they know they should ask for the tasks they want. Instead of having tasks dumped on them, they get to choose which they want. It's a simple technique that's very powerful.

But what if job enrichment isn't doing what you had hoped? If you feel like you've taken on additional responsibilities, have enriched your job in a number of ways, have talked to your manager about the situation, have applied for new positions listed on the job-posting system, and you still haven't gotten anywhere, you might have worked yourself into a box. A box is how people perceive you, and it often is connected to your job title. The prime example of this is the box that encircles the job of *"secretary."* No matter how many additional tasks a secretary takes on, she often is still perceived as a secretary.

If your old image is too firmly implanted, you may have to leave your organization. But first try all the techniques and strategies we have suggested. Many of our clients have been able to pop the top off the box and climb out, but some are locked in by bosses who don't want them to leave or stodgy organizations that can't see beyond job titles. If you have to leave, at least you'll be able to take with you all the new skills you acquired on the job.

Promoting Yourself within Your Own Organization

> *Lisa Wellington, a secretary who attended one of our workshops, agreed with every one of the statements under our "Am I Cut Out For The Corporate Climb?" quiz. She was unmarried, currently attending college, and eager to devote her life to work. Lisa completed her degree, started to dress more professionally, did her homework, had a career conversation with her boss, and knew she wanted to start her career in Human Resources. A HR job came up within the organization, Lisa applied for it, and she got it. "I am now," Lisa told us, "five years and two promotions later, the manager of Human Resources. No one even remembers that I was ever a secretary. I was able to get out of the box."*

Career Conversations with Your Manager

You don't appoint yourself to the position you want. Even if you think you're ready, even if you feel that you're the best candidate for a promotion, others have to see you as ready. And part of the perception of being ready is letting people know you're ready. Do not assume that your boss or your organization knows that you're in line for the next promotion or that prime position on the job-posting board. Far too many people act as if their bosses were mind readers.

Some of our clients complain about this. *"I'm dressing better, starting to take extra classes, and putting in additional hours at work,"* said one young man. *"But I don't see anyone noticing,"* he lamented. That's exactly our point. It's wonderful if you're starting to act like promotional material; it's just that you need to talk about it, too.

"Planning is bringing the future into the present so that you can do something about it now."
Alan Lakein

> "The man who is waiting for something to turn up might start on his shirt sleeves."
> Garth Heinrichs

That's why we recommend to our clients that they sit down and have a career conversation with their boss or manager. We know some of you may object to this. We've had participants in our workshops nearly jump out of their chairs when we suggest career conversations. *"Are you kidding me?"* they ask. *"It's not going to do me one bit of good. My boss is a total jerk."*

We understand that. Your boss or manager is either: a) your biggest career block; b) neutral to your career; or c) your greatest promoter and mentor. Only you know your relationship with your boss. And we definitely realize that many bosses are not going to help you with your career. They'd rather keep you where you are.

Why? Well, many bosses do not perceive themselves as *"growers of talent."* In an ideal world, that is what a boss is. From a boss's point of view, though, he or she doesn't have time to continually grow talent, and doesn't want to lose you. However, what these types of bosses don't understand is that they're going to lose their employees at some point anyway, regardless of how hard they try to keep them in their places.

If you truly have a boss who is your biggest career blocker, you need to make a lateral move in your organization or move out of your organization. This type of boss isn't changed by your desires. If your boss is either neutral to you or a help, great. The techniques we present will work for you.

You can't keep your career desires and wants a secret. You have to let your boss know what you want. However, you must do your homework before you attempt the career conversation. Answer the following questions to get you thinking about what a career conversation could do for you.

Promoting Yourself within Your Own Organization

What are the advantages of talking about your career with your manager?

_____
_____
_____

What reaction would you expect from your manager?

_____
_____
_____

What can you do to make the career conversation go smoothly?

_____
_____
_____
_____

Before you ask your manager or boss to sit down and talk with you, you need to think ahead and do some work. Your career conversation with your manager will be more productive, efficient, and satisfying if you have realistic expectations regarding what your manager could or should do to assist you with your career. What can your manager do?

He or she should be able to:

- Give you his or her undivided attention for a preset amount of time.

- Listen attentively and actively, and provide you with a *"sounding board"* for your ideas, goals, and plans.

- Ask for clarification and specifications on points that are not clear.

- Ask specific career questions that allow you to think about and sort out your specific career issues.

- Offer you feedback on your goals based on his or her knowledge of the organization's needs and goals.

- Offer you as many resources as possible regarding typical career paths, educational reimbursement programs, and training opportunities.

And what should your manager not be expected to do? Do not expect your manager to:

- Answer the question about exactly where you should go in your future career moves.

- Give you unlimited time to talk about your career.

- Know all of the organization's career paths, job descriptions, or current job openings.

- Know how you are feeling about the progress of your career without directly telling him or her about it.

> *One of our clients, Laura Block, took our "Am I Cut Out For The Corporate Climb?" quiz and discovered that she was willing to do everything listed except put in more than a forty-hour week. She had two small children at home. Because she was willing to do all the other things, Laura sat down and talked to her boss. "A new job was in the offering," Laura said, "and I had to decide whether or not to put my hat in the ring." Laura explained what she was more than willing to do, which was to work overtime on an occasional weekend, and she also explained that she needed to leave work on time during the week to pick up her kids. "I'm a quick and efficient worker," Laura explained, "and I felt that I could do the work in my time frame. My boss and I agreed that if I wasn't keeping up my part of the bargain, he would let me know and I would step down. Since I've started," she said, "he has had no complaints."*

For your career conversation to proceed as smoothly as possible, do your homework first and come to the conversation well prepared. We instruct our clients to go through the following three steps before they set up career conversations with their managers.

Step 1: Do some self-assessment

If you don't know where you're headed or what type of career interests you, don't expect your manager to. In our book, *Unlocking Your Career Potential*, we have readers analyze their desires, skills, and wants before coming up with career options. You should do the same. Read our book or take a career class at a local college. Only you can figure out where you want to end up.

> "We hear half of what is said, listen to half of what we hear, understand half of it, believe half of it, and remember half of that. So if you didn't get it the first time, ask again."
> Anonymous

Step 2: Project your career path (keeping your skills in mind)

Begin by listing the *"typical"* career-path options for your choice of career. Record your reactions and feelings about these options. Does one strike you as being a better match for your skills and interests? Also ask two people who know you and your work to tell you where they see you moving as your career progresses. The more input you have, the better.

Additionally, we encourage clients to join activities, committees, or projects that would put them in contact with people they wouldn't ordinarily meet. If you do this, you'll have a better chance of finding people who have skills similar to yours, but who haven't followed a typical career path. You might decide their choice is best for you.

Step 3: Prepare your thoughts ahead of time

Even if you've followed the previous two steps, you still need to collect what you've discovered and summarize it. If you've read *Unlocking Your Career Potential,* you'll have your career checklist to show your manager. In addition, write out your thoughts, questions, and feelings regarding possible career paths.

If you structure your career conversation, your manager will be impressed with your research and insights and be more willing to assist you. During the conversation, ask for resources you may need, such as career-path charts, job descriptions, other people to talk to, and/or training opportunities. Also ask for feedback. Be sure to listen as objectively as possible and let your manager speak without interruption.

Promoting Yourself within Your Own Organization

Many people try to manage their careers in a total vacuum. They don't seek feedback about their skills and abilities, so they never really know how well they did or in what areas they could improve. The only formal process for feedback is the performance evaluation. Yet most people don't get valuable feedback during a performance evaluation.

We want you to get feedback from both your manager *(during your career conversation)* and from others—be it peers, subordinates, or previous bosses. It only serves to further your career. But you may have to ask for feedback more than once, and you have to take the feedback in an appropriate manner and do something about it. If you are willing to do this, people will start to give you feedback and will give it as often as you request.

> *We helped one of our clients, Amanda Bennet, see the value of asking for and receiving feedback. Amanda worked for a major corporation that was going through a downsizing. "I am on the list of people who have yet to be chosen for a new position, and it scares me," she told us. Amanda had moved up fairly rapidly in the company, and now she didn't know what to do. We advised her to ask for feedback to discover why she wasn't being chosen. Amanda made appointments with three different people, two she had worked for and one she had worked with. "They were people I trusted, and also people who knew my work," Amanda shared with us. "I told them, 'I don't know if you know, but I haven't been selected yet. That's a cause of concern for me. I am literally asking you to give me honest feedback as to your perception why I have yet to be selected.' All three told me that I had excellent technical skills, but I did have some communication problems." On her own time, Amanda took a course in interpersonal communication and practiced improving her skills. She also made appointments with the three people who gave her the original feedback and told them how she had acted upon their suggestions. "I ended up getting a good position in the company, one that I really enjoy," Amanda said.*

> "The real risk is doing nothing."
> Denis Waitley &
> Remi L. Witt

If you seek feedback from people other than your manager, do it before your career conversation. It's a great preparation step if you act on it. Then make sure to set up your career conversation with your manager. One per year is optimal. This is not to be done during your performance evaluation. Most likely your manager or boss will not initiate a career conversation, so it's up to you. Every year you should ask yourself, *"Have I had a career conversation with my boss?"* If you haven't, do it.

What if you're fairly happy in your position and aren't really interested in moving up at this time? Maybe you were promoted a year ago, and your career path is the last thing on your mind. You still need feedback from your boss. There might be a new training class that you'd like to attend or you just might want to know what's going on. Many employees aren't even doing what their employers want them to and don't know it, simply because they don't check in. So schedule your conversation every year.

At the close of your career conversation, thank your manager for his or her time, and set up a tentative date for the next conversation. Then be sure to use the resources given to you. It will show your manager that you are serious about your career and that you value his or her input.

Marketing Strategies That Work

Throughout this book, we've talked a great deal about your marketing mix and the strategies you can use to self market successfully. Now we'd like to combine the various ideas, tips, and strategies into a list that you can use. Make it your to-do list to get what you want. It should become your personal self-marketing guide. Check which strategies apply to you; then prioritize them. And please feel free to add any self-marketing strategies that you can think of.

Promoting Yourself within Your Own Organization

_____ 1. Do a thorough self assessment
_____ 2. Ask three different people you trust for feedback about your skills and abilities.
_____ 3. Volunteer for any committee that interests you.
_____ 4. Take as many training classes as your organization will send you to.
_____ 5. Seek outside training activities on your own time.
_____ 6. Keep up with your business and industry through trade journals and newspapers.
_____ 7. Understand how you add value, and document that value through writing bullet statements.
_____ 8. Create an *"I love me"* file.
_____ 9. Have a yearly career conversation with your boss or manager.
_____ 10. Create a self-marketing script for all opportunities.
_____ 11. Look for all chances to enrich your job.
_____ 12. Share your bullet statements with your boss during your performance evaluation.
_____ 13. Check out the job-posting system in your organization and use it, when appropriate.
_____ 14. Make new contacts, and make time to keep up with your old contacts.
_____ 15. Make sure your personal image matches where you want to go.
_____ 16. Always look like a confident person *(look people in the eye, smile appropriately, shake hands firmly, look relaxed, and look like you have a sense of purpose)*.
_____ 17. If afraid of public speaking, take a course or join Toastmasters.
_____ 18. Continue to take advantage of all the opportunities in your daily life.
_____ 19. Do your homework to ensure that you are priced appropriately.
_____ 20. Join professional organizations in your field; attend their meetings.
_____ 21. Determine if you're ready for a lateral or upward move in your company.

It is our hope that you take these self-marketing strategies to heart and begin applying them to your career immediately. We've seen tremendous results from the clients who have done so. You can do the same.

Summary

Working your way up in your own organization can be done. First, however, it's critical that you determine if you really want to climb the corporate ladder. Not everyone is willing to pay the price. Some people decide to stay where they are, make a lateral move, or even choose realignment. Whatever your choice, make sure you prepare for and schedule a career conversation with your boss or manager at least once a year, and begin to enrich your job in every possible way. In so doing, you'll learn how to position yourself based on your own personal marketing mix. And don't forget to create your self-marketing to-do list. Many self-marketing options are available to you. Use them, and watch your career take off.

Marla Smith
CEO

Titles Currently Available in the Personal Growth and Development Collection

Managing Your Career in a Changing Workplace

Unlocking Your Career Potential

Marketing Yourself and Your Career

Making Career Transitions

Workshops

Dynamic and interactive in-house and public workshops are available from Richard Chang Associates, Inc. on a variety of personal, professional, and organizational development topics.

Additional Resources From Richard Chang Associates, Inc. Publications Division

Practical Guidebook Collection

Available through Richard Chang Associates, Inc., fine bookstores, and training and organizational development resource catalogs worldwide.

Quality Improvement Series
Continuous Process Improvement
Continuous Improvement Tools Volume 1
Continuous Improvement Tools Volume 2
Step-By-Step Problem Solving
Meetings That Work!
Improving Through Benchmarking
Succeeding As A Self-Managed Team
Satisfying Internal Customers First!
Process Reengineering In Action
Measuring Organizational Improvement Impact

Management Skills Series
Coaching Through Effective Feedback
Expanding Leadership Impact
Mastering Change Management
On-The-Job Orientation And Training
Re-Creating Teams During Transitions

High Performance Team Series
Success Through Teamwork
Building A Dynamic Team
Measuring Team Performance
Team Decision-Making Techniques

High-Impact Training Series
Creating High-Impact Training
Identifying Targeted Training Needs
Mapping A Winning Training Approach
Producing High-Impact Learning Tools
Applying Successful Training Techniques
Measuring The Impact Of Training
Make Your Training Results Last

Workplace Diversity Series
Capitalizing On Workplace Diversity
Successful Staffing In A Diverse Workplace
Team-Building For Diverse Work Groups
Communicating In A Diverse Workplace
Tools For Valuing Diversity

Training Products
Step-By-Step Problem Solving Tool Kit
Meetings That Work! Trainer's Kit
Continuous Improvement Tools Volume 1 Trainer's Kit
101 Stupid Things Trainers Do To Sabotage Success

Videotapes
Mastering Change Management**
Quality: You Don't Have To Be Sick To Get Better*
Achieving Results Through Quality Improvement*
Total Quality: Myths, Methods, Or Miracles**
   Featuring Drs. Ken Blanchard and Richard Chang
Empowering The Quality Effort**
   Featuring Drs. Ken Blanchard and Richard Chang

* Produced by American Media Inc.

Total Quality Video Series and Workbooks
Building Commitment**
Teaming Up**
Applied Problem Solving**
Self-Directed Evaluation**

** Produced by Double Vision Studios

Evaluation And Feedback Form

We need your help to continuously improve the quality of the resources provided through the Richard Chang Associates, Inc., Publications Division. We would greatly appreciate your input and suggestions regarding this particular book, as well as future book interests.

Thank you in advance for your feedback.

Title: _____

1. Overall, how would you rate your *level of satisfaction* with this book? Please circle your response.

Extremely Dissatisfied		Satisfied		Extremely Satisfied
1	2	3	4	5

2. What did you find *most* helpful?

   _____
   _____

3. What did you find *least* helpful?

   _____
   _____

4. What *characteristics/features/benefits* are most important to you in making a decision to purchase a book?

   _____
   _____

5. What additional *subject matter/topic areas* would you like to see addressed in future books from Richard Chang Associates, Inc.?

   _____
   _____

Name *(optional)*: _____

Address: _____

C/S/Z: _____   **Phone:** (___) _____

Please Fax Your Responses To: (714) 727-7007
Or Mail Your Response To: Richard Chang Associates, Inc.
15265 Alton Parkway, Suite 300, Irvine, CA 92618
Or Call Us At: (800) 756-8096